Introduction an[...]

Coal Mining
The history of the adjacent villages of Conisb[...]
development of coal mining as the rich Barnsley [...]
later 19th century. The major landowner, Mr Joh[...]
with a group of businessmen, led by John Buckingham Pope ana ᵣᵢₛ ₛₒᵣ...[...]
a lease for the Barnsley seam was signed in July 1862.

Denaby Main
In 1867 Denaby Main Colliery started producing coal and the first houses were erected the following year as a Colliery village - described as 'Pure Industrial Revolution' - was built. The first of several strikes followed in 1869 and the owners reacted by evicting the Miners and their families from the colliery houses they occupied. The men eventually won their battle for Union recognition and returned to work in September after the 6 months dispute.

Schools and a Cooperative Society were built and the Denaby Main Institute was opened in 1886. This followed the second major dispute when the men were 'locked-out' in 1885. The Company wanted to increase the ratio of large coal to small and eventually after more evictions and the lack of funds to support the strike by the Union the Company won the conflict.

Cadeby Main
The Denaby Main Colliery was the furthest East in the Yorkshire coalfield but this was to change when a sister pit was sunk just over a mile away near the small rural village of Cadeby. The shafts were sunk in 1891 and in 1893 a second Colliery, Cadeby Main began production.

Growth of Denaby Main village
Conisbrough had grown from these developments but the main growth was in Denaby Main itself as parallel streets of terraced houses were added. The houses were all similarly constructed as two up and two down dwellings from the same mud yellow, coal-blackened brick. Almost every street led down to the pit, without a tree or grass to be seen. In 1894 the Company built the Denaby Main Hotel, nicknamed the 'Drum', and miners received (and sometimes spent!) their wages in the Hotel each week.

The combined Pits were the most productive in Yorkshire, producing one and a half million tons of coal a year, all of it hewn and shovelled by hand. They were also the deepest and most dangerous.By the turn of the century 69 men had dies at Denaby Main and 12 more at Cadeby Main.

By the turn of the century the population of Denaby had grown to 2,670 with a large majority immigrating from the Midlands and Ireland. As the new found village struggled to find its identity, it gained notoriety in 1899, being described in a London magazine 'The Christian Budget' as 'The worst village in England'

Bag Muck Strike
1902 arrived and a dispute arose between the colliery owners and the miners over payment for the layer of dirt that miners had to remove before the coal could be mined - 'The Bag Muck'. Coal miners were paid on the amount of coal they extracted and - although at most collieries in South Yorkshire the men were paid a separate rate for removal of the 'bag muck'- not so at Denaby. In the months before the strike the faceworkers were coming across much

thicker seams of dirt and refused to remove the dirt without pay. The company drafted in labour to remove it and deducted the cost from the miner's wages. On 29th June 1902 the miners downed tools and struck. Six months later the striking miners were faced with eviction from their homes. This began in the heart of winter - 6th January 1903. A total of 750 families were evicted by 200 policemen, without trouble, over the next few days. The strike continued until March when the defeated Miners returned to work. The Company saw fit not to take back on some 500 of the 'troublemakers'.

King and Queen visit South Yorkshire
The troubled and dangerous times continued in the next decade and by 1912 another 34 men had perished through accidents in the Denaby pit and 47 more in the Cadeby pit. Industrial unrest in England had grown and was led by the miners and in March 1912 one million miners went on strike. After political concessions the miners returned to work the following month. The recently crowned King of England, George V, decided to visit South Yorkshire and the Earl Fitzwilliam at Wentworth House to see for himself the conditions of the working class, with particular emphasis on the Miners.

On July 8th the King and Queen visited Conisbrough Castle accompanied by flag-waving, cheering and elation. Hundreds of people had lined the streets and packed into the castle grounds, including many miners. Celebrations followed and the next day, at Cadeby Colliery, only 111 miners instead of the normal 500 turned up for work.

Cadeby Main Disaster
In the early hours of this fateful day, July 9th 1912, an explosion rent the workings and took the lives of 35 workmen. The rescue work began shortly afterwards and a second explosion between 10.30 and 11 a.m. took the lives of 53 of the rescuers. A further 3 men died as a result of the disaster, bringing the total lives lost to 91.

Commemoration
The purpose of this book is to tell through contempory articles, the story of the disaster, the visit of the King and Queen, the Inquiry which followed, the Heroes honoured, the Debate in Parliament and as much information as could be found of each of the victims and Heroes of the disaster. We appreciate this is not exhaustive and it you have any more information about the disaster or people please contact our Web site below.

The book contains Photographs, Newspaper Articles and many details from the Census of 1911, to build a picture of the people and the times and create a permanent record of this important event in our History.

Next year in 2012 will be the Centenary of the Disaster and this book has been compiled and sold to raise funds for a Memorial to the memory of the Miners. Thank you for buying a copy and your support.

Jim Beachill

Acknowledgements
To John Gwatkin for his painstaking research and the information provided. To all the people who have provided photographs. To the Mexborough and Swinton Times and Sheffield Telegraph for their comprehensive cover of the events; To the Doncaster Archives for their assistance and support; To the National Census for the glimpse of families in 1911. To David Bunce and Peter Davis for checking the information.

https://sites.google.com/site/conisbroughlocalhistory/home

Story Of The Disaster.

Mexborough & Swinton Times

The district has been thoroughly saddened and subdued this week by a great colliery disaster in our midst, the magnitude of which is yet scarcely to be realised and appreciated.

On Tuesday morning, at an hour variously estimated at between two and four, the south district of the Cadeby mine was rent by an explosion of terrific force, a deadly, silent tongue of destruction which swept along the main airway and sucked up all human life within range. The terrible and complete nature of the havoc it wrought may be gauged from the fact that of thirty-seven men who went down that district, thirty-five were killed outright, asphyxiated, scorched, burnt and torn to death. The other two wonderfully fortunate men were at the extreme edge of the district nearest to the pit-bottom, and so out of range of the mischief.

The Discovery
To these men : Albert Wildman, dataller of Ivanhoe Road, Conisbrough, and William Humphries, dataller of 38 Annerley Street, Denaby Main, is left the telling of the tale, which after all is very incomplete.

Except that the two men were very near the centre of the disaster shortly after it occurred, and saw the riot and ruin which the explosion brought in it's train, they have not been able to tell us much more than might have been safely left to the imagination.

Albert Wildman

They were so far from the seat of destruction – nearly a mile – that the blast was reduced to a 'puff of air' when it reached them, but they were both experienced miners – Humphries had been seventeen years in the pit – and they knew what it meant. They cast about uneasily for signs of mischief, anxiously they enquired all round the neighbouring district, and then, not without an inward tremor for the ominous silence which had bore within it suggestions of deadliness calculated to give pause to the boldest, they pushed forward.

William Humphries

An Ordeal.
"All honour to these men." They do not appear conspicuously in the newspaper accounts as heroes, but they were suddenly faced with an ordeal of the kind which heroes undergo. They did their best. They ascertained as an absolute fact that there had been a serious explosion, and that men had been killed. There was no guesswork about it. They went to see.

The Narrative.
I was, luckily, the first Pressman to get told a reliable account of the tragedy which virtually accounted for almost eighty lives, and it was William Humphries who told me the story of an awful discovery in the hideous blackness of a sub- teranean slaughterhouse. He told me in quiet level tones, what he had seen and heard, giving

me a plain, matter-of-fact narrative, which was the more impressing because it lacked obvious exaggerations.

He told me how the little party he and Wildman, Joseph Farmer, Jack Bullock, and Deputy Fisher crept forward into the hollow stillness of the graveyard, past the level where the tubs were smashed and the girders twisted till they came upon the body of Martin Mulrooney of Mexborough, a dataller. Half the party went forward and the other half went back to give the alarm, and speedily the colliery above and below was alive with excitement and eager enthusiasm for rescue.

No Chance Of Life.

But there never was any question of rescues. The appearance of poor Martin Mulrooney, stretched in the dust at the end of the storm centre told us that no man could have been within range of that fierce sheet of flame and lived. Still, with the air sweet and good, and the roof apparently sound, a free current of air going right through, a few of the men went on with the desperate hope of finding life somewhere among the shattered ruins. It was a vain hope and a fleeting glance at one of the men recumbent around was good enough for a certificate of death. They were lying all over the gallery, some were in natural attitudes, others in that protective posture which is said to accompany any death by burning, and others like Mulrooney, buried face downwards in heaps of soft dust.

Recumbent Statues.

All were badly burned, some horribly scarred, while others, mercifully spared disfiguration, were merely bronzed, and looked statuesque with their stiff extended arms and their hard solid-looking flesh. In eight cases out of ten, the fire had completely shaved the hair of the victims from their heads, and the burns of those poor fellows was weird and inhuman. All the men, of course, had died of asphyxiation, but their burns would have accounted for a very heavy proportion of them apart from the deadly gas, and in some cases the men were badly cut about the head and face.

Rescue Work Begun.

It would be about six o'clock before the management could get to work on the recovery of the bodies, and the splendid rescue teams attached to the two collieries were down the pit within half-an-hour, while in another half-hour the Wath rescue-station had sent over a motor car full of men and was standing by to send as much assistance as five collieries would be likely to require.

Gathering Of Forces.

Sergeant-Instructor Winch was with it, and marshalled

the rescue operations. Mr. Charles Bury, the manager of the mine and Mr. Harry Witty, agent of the collieries, sprang up from nowhere. While the former went underground the latter stayed above to superintend the thousand and one details which required instant attention, and to stem the rapidly rising confusion which threatened to overwhelm the officials.

Mr. W.H. Chambers, the managing director of the company was summoned from Newcastle and Mr. W.H. Pickering, Divisional Inspector of Mines, came hurrying up from Doncaster at seven o'clock, with his assistant Mr. Gilbert Tickle, while from the other direction the senior inspector, Mr. H.R. Hewitt, of Sheffield, and the number of official inspectors was shortly made up by the arrival of Mr. H. M. Hudspeth and Mr. H.R.R. Wilson, of Leeds.

The rescue teams got to work quickly and quietly and the ventilation being good and sound their appliances were not needed after the first trial.

A Ghastly Procession.

At nine o'clock began the ghastly procession of the dead. Slowly and with reverence they were carried out of the pit-mouth down the two long gantries in full view of the thousands of alarmed onlookers. From seven o'clock until nine the great crowds had gradually accumulated in the roads leading to the pit-yard but all was completely quiet then, for no one knew anything definite.

People merely amused themselves with conjecture and were inclined to regard the rumoured explosion as another of the mare's nests for which many colliery 'explosions' are often taken as fitting subjects. But the appearance of that first corpse on the top of the tall gantry was enough for the onlookers. A gasp of horror flew around, and swift as the message of the beacon light, the whole of the district was appraised of the horror within their midst.

A Terrible July Day.

The memory of that terrible Tuesday will live for countless generations. No pen can draw a picture of the horror of it all. The golden sunlight of a warm July day bathed the countryside in an atmosphere of peace and joy, but the ill fated colliery stood out from the hillside of Cadeby black and stern and sinister and forbidding.

The flags which had floated from it's headgears the previous day to welcome a King and his Consort, were gone and no touch of colour relieved the great gaunt tombstone.

All that long black terrible day the bodies took their solemn journey down that awful gantry. Men who went to their work hearty and strong at night, came back stiff and cold at noon, men who gallantly rushed to the rescue at noon were gently shunted twisted and lifeless on the slabs at night-fall. The day was bright and balmy elsewhere.

Death In The Wind.
Here there was a cold shudder in the air, and a whisper of death in the wind. The crowd, which had flocked into the place from miles around in the heat of the afternoon grew and swelled until, at seven o'clock there must have been a great congregation of not less than eighty thousand. Every one was a mourner, and in all that multitude scarcely a sound seemed to be raised. Every where was grey stolid grief, and only when you mingled with the crowd did you detect here the soft weeping of a widow, and there the low fearful mutterings of a father whose strong bright son was no more. Anything more impressive and depressing one could not well imagine.

The Crowning Disaster.
It is a matter of history that the crowning disaster, overshadowing even the holocaust of the morning, came at half past eleven, when a second explosion came along in the centre of the former mischief, and descended amongst the rescuers as they were in the act of taking bodies away, wiped them almost completely out – a fine, gallant force, which included one of the most brilliant mines' inspectors in the world, and two of his devoted colleagues, a manager of a mine, and four or five leading officials.
The slaughter of the morning was outdone, and the death-roll sprang, in the twinkling of an eye, from thirty-five to seventy-five. The stunning horror of the thing paralysed all movement for a time, and the grief and sorrow, which held that great crowd in one common bond deepened and accentuated. Forty more victims meant hundreds more mourners.

No Respecter Of Persons.
And while we all sorrowed for the poor Dicks, Toms, and Harrys, who had met their deaths, we were shocked inexpressively at the rude impartiality of the Sinister Angel, who, respecting no person, cut off Mr. Pickering, Mr. Tickle, Mr. Hewitt, Mr. Douglas Chambers, Mr. Herbert Cusworth, and, as we then believed, Mr. Charles Bury, every one a man of high repute and inestimable value in the coal-mining industry.

It seemed hard to realise that men who were accustomed to rule and control the wild elements which wreck coal-raising should themselves be struck dead by these rebellious forces. Slowly and by degrees we realised it. The procession of bodies was a little quicker, and now and then we marked the progress of one of these more distinguished victims as we saw the small despondent groups of men escorting their biers.

Personal Tragedies.
Mr. Edward Chambers, the manager of Cortonwood, and father of Mr. Douglas Chambers, was on the scene early in the morning, and was hard at work below when he lost his boy.

Another personal tragedy who was contained in the pathetic circumstances was that Mr. Basil Pickering, the manager of Wath Main, who was among the rescuers at the time of the second explosion, and who helped to carry his father out.

There were several remarkable escapes in the second explosion. Sergeant Winch and a man named Lawrence of the Denaby Rescue Party, were the only ones who survived from the Denaby & Cadeby Rescue Teams, the remainder being wiped out. The Cadeby team, I am told, was practically the same as that which performed before the King at Windsor Park.

A Remarkable Escape.
Sergeant Winch's story was brief and plain and graphic. He said that all seemed right, they were all perfectly comfortable. The air was good, and there was nothing to suggest further peril. That being so, he and Lawrence turned back a little way to replenish their lamps, and were about to rejoin their party, when there came the blinding flash of the second explosion, and they were thrown to the ground. They picked themselves up and ran for dear life. They were practically unhurt, but it was a very close thing. Those two were among the first to make a second attempt at rescue, and, to do them full justice, were undeterred by their grisly experience.

Blissful Ignorance.
Still on the subject of personal tragedies, it is noteworthy that the wife of the doomed Divisional Inspector rode the greater part of the way from York to Doncaster with an evening paper containing an account of her husband's death before it occurred to her to open it and read it., an instance of blissful ignorance for which it is doubtful whether the lady is thankful. She had been playing a brilliant tennis game at Newcastle for Yorkshire against Northumberland.

What They Missed.
There were several remarkable escapes from the second explosion, if providential diversions can be described as escapes. Three of the younger officials, Messrs. Herbert Williamson, Tom Soar, and Norman Walker were prevented from being in the thick of the disaster by some trifling circumstance or other occurring just a minute or two beforehand. Mr.

Witty himself would, in the ordinary course, have been there, and, as soon as the crowd above heard of the explosion, with the wholesale slaughter it had brought in it's train, they, knowing the bold and enterprising nature of the gentleman, instantly credited him with being among the slain, and so set up a disconcerting rumour. The fact of the matter was, so far as I can gather, that Mr. Witty stayed at the pit-head in response to the request of Mr. Pickering, that he should remain behind to see to things there. He is supposed to have made a jesting remark to the effect that it was no use them all risking it. I further understand that Mr. Witty was about to call Mr. Pickering out of the pit in order that he might fulfil his Royal engagement, when, before he could do so, he was met with the urgent request, " Come at once, pit blown up again," and he went down to help recover Mr. Pickering's body.

Mr. Bury In Desperate Straits.
The second explosion brought down a very large fall of roof. Mr. Redmayne, His Majesty's Chief Inspector of Mines, speaking to me on Wednesday, admitted it was a very large one, but described it as the kind of fall which usually follows an explosion. It is, however, variously estimated at from one hundred to two hundred tons in weight. Many of the poor fellows in the rescue party were caught in this huge fall, and their case was at once hopeless. The others, who were further in advance, were cut off by the fall, and were promptly gassed. These included Mr. Chambers, and Mr. Pickering. Mr. Charles Bury, in whose fate tremendous interest was taken, appears to have been protected by a special providence. He was one of the earliest to be recovered, and he was found to be in a very bad way indeed, though his limbs were protected from the fall by the bodies of two other men which were heaped up over him. He was all but gone when taken to the surgery, but the doctors tackled him gallantly, and fought desperately for a very valuable life. Dr. Forster was particularly prominent in resuscitation, though the other doctors who were periodically in attendance – Dr. J.J. Huey, of Mexborough, Dr's Feroze and McArthur, of Denaby Main – did very valuable work in other directions. Dr. Forster, however, remained with Mr. Charles Bury the whole of the night in the Denaby Fullerton Hospital, working strenuously at the feeble, flickering life to keep it going.

The gravest fears were entertained of this genial gentleman's condition, but reports were distinctly more encouraging twenty-four hours later. The greatest anxiety was displayed throughout the entire district on the score of the Cadeby manager's fate, for to lose Mr. Charles Bury meant to lose not only one of the cleverest mine managers in the north of England, but one of the most genial souls who ever passed a merry hour.

Mr. Cusworth Gone.

8

When the confusion and terror had cleared away, and all was temporarily safe, the decimated little party turned and examined itself, and found itself short of a number of other valuable men. Herbert Cusworth, the capable under-manager of the colliery, was nowhere to be found. Here was another distinct loss. Mr. Cusworth it will be remembered, came to Cadeby from Hoyland Silkstone in May of last year, in succession to Mr. Tom Mosby, who went to Maltby. Since he has been at Cadeby he has done extremely well, and has been a valuable right hand to Mr. Bury, as he was in the cricket field also. Only the other Saturday he knocked up a sparkling sixty-two against Swinton. He was a bluff, but genial and pleasant man, thoroughly interested in all that interested the village, but especially in sport and ambulance work. He was a sound cricketer, and he was also closely connected with the Denaby United Football Club in the capacity of general secretary. Poor Cusworth had gone. That fact was ascertained very early. Such appears to have been the deadly nature of the place that all who were not to be seen in the flesh could be put down as not merely missing, but dead.

Rescue Teams Wiped Out.
Then the whole of the Denaby and Cadeby rescue teams, with the exception of Sergeant Winch and Lawrence, were wiped out of existence, and they included some fine fellows, men who had a fortnight before excited the admiration of a King by their skill in just the kind of work in which they were engaged when they met their doom. There was William Humphries, captain of the Cadeby team, and a nephew of that William Humphries who discovered the original explosion ; the was Jack Carlton, William Summerscales, and the rest, all good men who died fighting.

Another Instance Of Providence.
Another loss is that of poor Sidney Ellis, a third officer in the Ambulance Brigade, surveyor at the colliery, and one of the foremost men in the rescue party. He, with Cusworth, Charlie Prince, Jackson, and seven or eight others, lay buried beneath that huge fall. A cheerful soul was Ellis, and a fine sport. He had a taste for music. Occasionally you could get him to sing at one of the convivials they were always having in that happy and gay village, and he could sing a good song in a good voice. But how abominably he forgot to bring his music. To the writer, who knows some of these men as his own brothers, it is indeed trying work setting down the history of their destruction.

Charlie Prince, who was also hopelessly buried, was one of the smartest and most promising youngsters in the pit, and his death is being most widely mourned throughout Denaby and Mexborough. It is tragic to reflect that there was also a pathetic might-have-been in this case, for I

understand that on Tuesday morning, Prince, who is deeply interested in the Boy Scout movement, was taking a troop from Mexborough to Doncaster, en route for Hickleton Hall, there to line up for the approach of the King. Hearing of the explosion, he broke his journey at Conisbrough, and his Boy Scouts went forward. He joined the rescue party, and was one of the first to be killed. The sympathy of the whole district is with his sister, Miss E. Prince, of the staff of the Mexborough Secondary School, and with his younger brother Walter, who was down the mine at the time, and who refused to leave until he was absolutely convinced that his brother's plight was hopeless. When the fate of the poor lad became known beyond doubt, the heart-broken brother and sister repaired to their home in Nottinghamshire. Mr. Prince and Mr. Douglas Chambers were both members of the Denaby Tennis Club, which is thus bereaved of two of it's most valued members.

The Old Brigade.
Another victim who has rendered valuable service in the Cadeby mine and who was killed with the rescue party, is Eli Croxall, another true Denaby-ite, jovial and hospitable, and a thoroughly good fellow. I could go on almost indefinitely through the list, calling attention to the sterling qualities of men who will be sorely missed in the days to come, but the recitals would be too long, and the reading it would be too painful to permit myself the indulgence.

Long before we had recovered from the crushing blow of the second terrific calamity, messages of sympathy began to pour into the place, and were posted up one by one on the railings of the general office. The gracious, kindly message of the King and Queen was the first of all, and then, immediately following the spread of the news of the second explosion, came a long sympathetic wire from the Home Secretary, who referred particularly to the great loss sustained in the death of Mr. Pickering and his colleagues. There were messages from the Mayors of Rotherham and Barnsley, and afterwards pouring in thick and fast from the West Riding Miners' Permanent Relief Society, from the Yorkshire Miners' Association – delivered in person by Mr. John Dixon

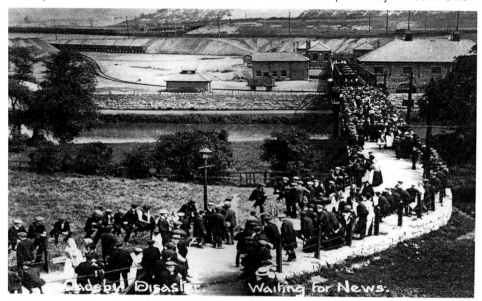

Cadeby Disaster. Waiting for News.

and Mr. Sam Roebuck, from the Mayor of Sheffield, the Master Cutler, General and Lady Copley, of Sprotborough Hall, the Archbishop of York, the Countess of Yarborough, and many others.

The huge shifting crowds stared dumbly at them, and wondered how they were going to make up to them for the loss of those they held so dear. It is to the lasting credit of the clergy, Established and Nonconformist, that they busied themselves throughout the devastated neighbourhood spreading any spiritual solace and comfort wherever they could. The Vicars of Denaby, and Conisbrough, and Mexborough, with Father Kavanagh of Denaby, the Primitive Methodist minister of Mexborough and others, were to be seen visiting darkened homes all the livelong day.

Huge Gathering.
At seven o'clock in the evening there were more people assembled within a radius of a quarter-of-a-mile of the Cadeby Colliery than there ever were before, or probably ever will be again. The footbridge over the Conisbrough railway station and the lane leading to the glass-works, each converging on the direct lane over the river bridge to the pit-yard, were packed from side to side with people. They scarcely spoke to each other. They just stared in dumb bewilderment at the colliery and it's environs, and at the occasional corpse which came down the pit gantry.

One Bright Ray.
By the time Mr. Frank Allen, the District Coroner, arrived from Mexborough, to open the inquest, sixty-five bodies had been placed in the pay-station ; but before that, and at about half past seven, there came two visitors who by their presence shed the one bright ray upon the awful gloom of a disastrous day. The King and Queen came to mingle their tears with those of a sorrowing people ! It was hard to realise that their Majesties were actually in the midst of this great debacle of death and ruin ; but such was the case. They had motored over from Wentworth on the completion of the day's duties in company with Earl Fitzwilliam and Lord Stamfordham.

There were only two cars and they came into the village by way of Hill Top and through Conisbrough. The crowd realised suddenly as the cars slowed up before the colliery offices who the illustrious visitors were, and made a mad rush in that direction. They commenced cheering their Majesties, but the King, with a sublime expression on his face which told of the great grief which consumed him, raised his hand as if in reproof of the mistimed plaudits of the multitude, and the cheering died away, giving place to murmured benedictions.

Royal Sorrow Mingles With People's Grief.
Their Majesties were received in the

colliery offices by Mr. W.H. Chambers and Mr. J.R.R. Wilson, both dishevelled and begrimed by their labours underground, and at the request of the King and Queen these gentlemen supplied them with particulars of the disasters. The King inquired particularly as to the fate of his faithful servants, the Government inspectors, and was tremendously touched by the recital of all that had happened. The interview did not last more than ten minutes or quarter-of-an-hour, but it was extremely painful while it was on.

The King looked pale and sorrowful as he appeared with his Queen at the top of the colliery office steps, and the Queen, without restraint at all, shed the tears of a mother, wife and daughter. Another moment, and they were gone on their way through Conisbrough to Wentworth, but they left behind them in that brief visit a great and lasting impression throughout the whole of the British Empire, for George and Mary had shown the people that they could not only rejoice with them and receive their homage, but could weep with them, and visit them in their affliction. The visit was epoch-making, and will make a magnificent piece of twentieth century history.

All-Night Vigil
After the several identifications that were brought forward, Mr. Allen went across to the Colliery Offices to sign the necessary death certificates permitting the removal of bodies, but no bodies at all were removed on Tuesday night.   The first to go was that of Mr. Pickering on Wednesday morning when his widow had it conveyed to Doncaster.

The jury and the little army of Pressmen, the latter numbering something near fifty, left the inquest room and the colliery for the night at ten o'clock. Not so the crowd. They hung around for hours afterwards. Scores of families, I am told, kept an all-night vigil, doing nothing but simply standing and staring at the pay-station with the dimly-lit windows, behind which sixty-five white sheeted forms lay stiff and stark.
Fortunately it was a hot July night, and the hungering crowds suffered no material discomfort from the weather. So ended the ninth of July, the blackest day South Yorkshire since Old Oaks and Lundhill.

A Third Explosion.

Tuesday's Rescue Volunteers
When we returned early on Wednesday morning to delve into further details of the cataclysm, it was to be met with the despairing intelligence that there had occurred another explosion during the night, at about half-past-three in fact, and that the rescue workers, in endeavouring to shut off the deadly south district by brick-stoppings in the intake and return airways, had narrowly escaped another catastrophe, for

the explosion blew out the stoppings, and they had to scamper for their lives

Two of them sustained serious injury, and I believe one of the rescuers, a man named Hulley, who was included in the Windsor Park rescue team, but fortunately not in the one which shared the fate of the forty on Tuesday afternoon, had a wonderfully narrow escape from death. By seven o'clock the stoppings had been restored, and thanks to a periodical inspection of them, were not disturbed for the remainder of the day, though of course there came along an inevitable rumour that more men were entombed later in the day.

An Interview.
At about ten o'clock information was very scarce, and the company of Pressmen chafed sorely at the non-committal attitude of the officials of the colliery, who declined to give information or facilities for getting it, so that the more erstwhile of the correspondents almost broke out into open rebellion, Mr. Chambers was however, good enough to grant me an interview, and with him I met Mr. Redmayne, His Majesty's Chief Inspector of Mines for Great Britain, and Mr. J. R.R. Wilson, of Leeds, who on the death of Mr. Pickering, became acting Divisional Inspector. They explained to me the present condition of the mine, but frankly confessed their inability to give any forecast of the future conditions or what was likely to be accomplished within, at any rate, the next few weeks.

Condition Of The Mine.
"The management," said Mr. Redmayne, "are exercising every possible precaution to prevent air from getting to the affected area and by that action they hope to suppress the mischief, whatever it is. The stoppings in the intake and return airways will be periodically examined by bands of skilled men."

" It is not," he said in reply to my inquiry," a particularly hazardous duty, but it calls for the shrewd judgement of trained men. I am departing almost immediately for London, where I shall report fully to the Home Secretary and make arrangements for the Home Office inquiry."

The Fall Of Roof.
All three gentlemen agreed that the mischief was caused without doubt by explosions, and that the original disaster was not due, as had been suggested by another official, to other causes. " The second explosion," said Mr. Redmayne, " brought down a very large roof fall. How large I cannot say, but just such a fall as explosions do bring down."

Death Toll Of Eighty-One.
Mr. Chambers informed me that at that time (Wednesday noon), there were seventy-one bodies recovered, and there were five living patients in hospital. There were to his knowledge three bodies under the fall, those of Mr. Cusworth, Mr. Ellis, and Mr. Prince. There might be more, but not many more. This number was amended to ten as late as Wednesday night, which brings the death toll up to eighty-one.
The bodies were not likely to be recovered until Thursday, I was given to understand, in the interests of the safety of the mine. This was all the official information then available, though Mr. Chambers did courteously express a willingness to supply all essential information which was due to the public.

Another " Might Have Been."

When questioned by another interviewer, as to the cause of the accident, Mr. Chambers said," All I can say is it is most mysterious."

Mr. Wilson, when questioned, was also at a loss for the explanation of the accident. I don't know whether the public know, he went on, " but there is absolutely no shot-firing in this pit. Another matter the public might hang on to is the presence of electricity, but there is no chance of this explosion being linked to electricity in any shape. These are the chief dangers and it cannot be either," and in a brief reference to the fate of his colleague, he significantly replied," Why I am not among them is because the telephone did not happen to work early enough this morning."

The Archbishop In The Homes.

There were extinguished visitors to the village during the morning. Viscount and Viscountess Halifax, with two ladies, drove over from Hickleton Hall, and made enquiries as to the latest developments. Mr. J. Buckingham Pope, chairman of the Denaby and Cadeby Colliery Company, arrived from London at 11-30, and just before His Grace the Archbishop of York had motored over from Wentworth in company with the Hon. Henry Fitzwilliam and Capt. F. Brooke, and after leaving a message of sympathy at the Colliery Offices, which was duly posted up, proceeded to the pit-yard in company with Mr. G. Wilkie, the secretary of the company, and the Vicar of Conisbrough, the Rev. W.A. Strawbridge. He held a short but an extremely impressive and touching service in the mortuary and at the pit-head. These were attended by all the available officials and men who were at hand, and prayers were offered for the solace and comfort of the bereaved, while the Archbishop addressed to the men strengthening counsel and guidance.

When he left the pit-yard, without returning to the colliery offices, he made a tour of Denaby Main and Conisbrough, and visited the homes of several of the bereaved families, carrying with him brightness and refreshment, and speaking to many of the poor people words of comfort and hope.

As the visit of the King and Queen had been the one bright spot on Tuesday, so was the visit of the Archbishop the one alleviating feature of the gloom and despair of Wednesday. After he had completed his round, he had a conference with the Vicars of Denaby Main, Conisbrough and Mexborough, with regard to the funeral arrangements, and some interesting decisions were arrived at.

Great Massed Funeral On Friday.

Most of the bodies were being busily coffined in the pay-station at the time, the colliery company supplying the major batch of coffins, thirty or forty of which appeared on drays early on Wednesday morning.

Eight sextons were hard at work on a special plot of ground in the Denaby churchyard, where it is anticipated something like sixty burials will take place on Friday afternoon at three o'clock, all of them, save for a few, which will take place in family graves, in the specially allotted portion.

It has been arranged that the Archbishop shall

conduct the first part of what will be a tremendously impressive service in the Denaby Main Parish Church, and that being the case, it is anticipated that the whole of the families of the victims will fall in with the arrangements.

The Conisbrough internments will be taken separately at Conisbrough, and the Mexborough interments, of which there are less than half a dozen, may be included in those at Denaby.

It has been arranged, that if the relatives are agreeable, the coffins shall be placed in the church and seats allotted for each company of mourners.
After the services in the Church, the committals will be taken in various parts of the ground by the Rev. F.S. Hawkes and his assistant curate, the Rev. J. Tunnicliffe, and by the Vicar of Mexborough, the Rev. W.H.F. Bateman R.D., and his assistant curates, the Rev.'s S.H. Lee and S.H. Spooner.
The climax of it will be the funeral oration in the Denaby Main Parish Church on Sunday night. His Grace is indeed a man of deeds. He is nothing if not thorough.

A Drab Atmosphere.
Wednesday was lacking in general incident, a dull apathy seemed to have descended over the neighbourhood from the very outbreak of the trouble and it required a great deal to lift it. A tour of the village of Denaby Main made up a very dreary pilgrimage. Up one street and down another you saw nothing but the hideous monotony of drawn blinds and women standing discussing the accident in the street, relieved in sinister fashion here and there by the sight of a coffin being transferred from the colliery ambulance into a house or by over-hearing hackneyed street-door philosophy. But on Wednesday morning about half-past-nine, there cropped up one little incident which served to show the real temper of the crowd, hidden as it was beneath the phlegm and lethargy of a stunned populace.

Uncouth Photographer Punished.
Three women were returning from the pay-station, where they had been to identify relatives, and as they appeared in great trouble and were weeping in concert, a callous young Press photographer, scenting only a startling picture, and without any regard for the finer feelings, stepped right into their paths and held his camera in front of their faces while he got a steady 'snap'. The crowd promptly smashed his camera, and nearly smashed him.

The Final Offices. Thursday morning.
There was very little fresh information to be had at Cadeby on Thursday morning. But in comparison with the other two days the place was wonderfully quiet and deserted. The explanation was obvious, the families of the victims were busy, quietly making preparations for the burial of their dead on the morrow.
Down at the pay-station a company of nursing women were doing excellent work in coping with the laying-out of the bodies prior to the process of their coffining. When the disaster first broke out the women were at once on the scene together with some auxiliaries from Wath, but they were sent back. They were not wanted then. But they were sadly wanted in the two succeeding days, when the bodies had to be prepared for their grave clothes, and they worked splendidly under the ghastly conditions and suffering the continuous ordeal of unpleasant stenches. Under the sweating heat of the July sun the mortuary attendants had hard work to keep the

advance of decomposition in something like decent check, and the pay-station seemed to ooze with the persistent odour of disinfectants. Gradually, however, the coffins received their appointed burdens, and by Thursday afternoon most of them were safely lodged in the homes of the victims. There is a general air of desolation and idleness about the district, which seems to suggest that there never will be any work at Cadeby colliery. At Denaby colliery, since Tuesday, work has been carried out in a desultory fashion, but, practically speaking, there has been nothing done anywhere.

I am told that it is likely that Cadeby colliery will re-open for work next Monday, but it is quite impossible to say what will be, or indeed, can be, done with the devastated district where lie the bodies of ten men still missing from the mortuary. Those bodies will have to be recovered as early as is possible, consistent with the safety of the mine, after which a tremendous fall of roof will have to be made good, and the whole length of the district covered by the explosion will have to be thoroughly repaired after it has been made accessible by the extinction of the fire. It is hardly likely that for a month or six-weeks at least, there will be any goal-getting in this South District, which bears a sinister name for evermore.

Sorry Time For Officials.
It has been a sorry time for the officials of the Company. They have been racked and riven by desperate relatives, importunate Pressmen, and excited messages from the pit, until they have scarcely known what to do or how to do it. A good deal of the confusion which early set in was doubtless due to the absence in Newcastle, of the president genius, who, however, came as quickly as he could. Doubtless, if the work of the officials had been classified, things would have gone much more smoothly, but a luckless official setting forth on a mission might, before he could accomplish it, have ten other missions thrust upon him.

It was a long time before the confusion and chaos, even in a well-organised office like this, could be reduced to order.

The dreadful aftermath of funerals opened on Friday, and for a day or two Denaby and Conisbrough seemed to live in an atmosphere of varnished coffins and black-coated processions. It was dreary and depressing in the extreme and a great sigh of relief went up when, by Wednesday, most of the victims who were to be buried locally had reverently disappeared to their last resting places. Picture two mining villages with blinds drawn for a week and you can then imagine a good deal of the rest. The same unnatural stillness which has never lifted from the area since the disaster prevailed on Friday and Saturday, whilst the clergy were busy performing their office and great though the grief and the bitterness was, one simply longed for some diversion to relax the terrible tension of quiet, patient, and stony suffering.

Sexton's Busy.

There were sixteen funerals at Denaby and ten at Conisbrough on Friday, while on Saturday there were eight at Conisbrough and six at Denaby, and on Sunday five at Conisbrough and one at Denaby. Most of the funerals at Denaby were taken by the Established Church, but nine were interred with Roman Catholic rites, including the body of Mr. Charles Bury, the last, and probably the greatest and most deeply mourned victim of the disaster, who was the ninth.

At Conisbrough twenty-five graves were made in the cemetery for the victims of the disaster, and they were dug by fourteen sextons, with Mr. A. Hodgson, the cemetery caretaker, in charge. The work all round in connection with the funerals was excellently and swiftly done. Eight sextons were kept busily at work in the Denaby cemetery, and of course a large number of victims are being buried by their friends in different parts of the country. On Thursday, Friday and Saturday the railway company were busily despatching the bodies, principally via Doncaster, and coaches were kept constantly in the sidings for the purpose.

The First Funeral.

The first funeral to be taken at Conisbrough was that of poor Cyrus Schofield, at ten o'clock in the morning, and the first at Denaby was at mid-day, that of Charles Fletcher. From then onwards the processions were continuous, and there was a following of comrades and workmen for each one. The big feature of Friday's funerals was of course the obsequies of Mr. Douglas Chambers' funeral, whose loss in the second explosion is so deeply and widely deplored, and which creates a vacancy in the managership of the Denaby Main Colliery. He was a Superintendent in the Ambulance Brigade, and all that fine brigade could do, to make the funeral impressive and surround it with a halo of respect they did.

A Terrible Storm.

The ladies of the family were not well enough to undergo the ordeal of attending the internment, though it must be said that terrible as the blow has been, they have sustained it with fortitude throughout. A very dramatic feature of the funeral day was the terrible thunderstorm which broke right over Denaby and Conisbrough at the conclusion of Mr Douglas Chambers funeral, and which would give any amount of scope to the imagination of the superstitious. It was so fierce and prolonged as to cause considerable delay in carrying out the remaining internments, and one funeral party was actually caught in the thick of the storm when standing beside the grave in the cemetery, so that they were soaked to the skin with a tremendously heavy downfall. The delay occasioned at Denaby was so considerable that the last funeral was not completed until half-past eight o'clock, when the clergy of Denaby, who, during the day had been assisted by the clergy from Mexborough, wound up what is probably the saddest and heaviest days of their lives.

Survivors Stories

Sheffield Daily Telegraph

Dead bodies lying all around

Horace Dokinfield, miner, aged 21, who lives in Tickhill Road, Denaby, told me he was one of the first four to go down the pit with stretchers.

'I got down to the scene of the disaster about 10 minutes past six. I saw huge falls of rubbish and dead bodies lying all around. The sight down there was terrible. Some of the bodies were shattered all to pieces. You could hardly tell they had been men. From that until now (3.30) I have been bringing out the dead and I have had enough. I can stand no more of it. It looked as if most of the men had been killed instantly – just snuffed out. I should not think there was a single one of them living two minutes after the explosion took place. Six or seven horses were lying about too.

I was in the main plane making for some more bodies when I heard a loud report and a gust of wind swept up the plane, and the roof came tumbling down. I ran back in time and I believe that all the ambulance men were as lucky as myself. This second explosion took place at exactly the same spot as the first. It had done them all – Government inspectors, company officials, rescuers, and miners alike had been stamped out. '

Survivors thrilling story

The man who last saw Mr. Pickering and the company with him alive was Percy Murgatroyd, a young married miner. It was with difficulty he told me of his awful experience for he was on the verge of collapse. This is what he told me;

I was one of the first rescuers to go down the mine. There were three other men in our party. We got to the point where the explosion had taken place, and never shall I forget the horrible sight which met my eyes. The bodies were shattered most awfully. I cannot bear to talk about it. Of course we wore respirators and we worked hard for many hours.

I should think it was about 11 o'clock. At that time 28 bodies had been got out and I joined a* little exploring party, assisted by Mr. Bury, general manager of the mine, Mr Pickering Government inspector and two or three other gentlemen of mining fame, but I don't know who they were. We were trying to find out what was the cause of the explosion. There is the rather important point. I was the only man who wore a respirator. The air was very good and there really seemed to be no need for one, but it was business to penetrate into any part of the workings that they might instruct me to, and so it was advisable that I should wear one. There might be places where it would be dangerous to be without. A rescue party consisting, I should think of about 30 men passed quite close to us and were busy about their work.

The Air Trembled

Murgatroyd went on: We were talking quite casually when all at once there was a trembling of the air. We had no time to seek a place of safety. The explosion was upon us. I am rather misty as to details but I can remember a fearful roar, and then clouds of dust and smoke were surging all around. I have a very confused recollection of what happened; I think I must have been stunned for the moment.

When I came to myself the air was so thick that, although I had a powerful electric lantern in my hand, I could not see more than a few inches in front of my face. I used my respirator and my head got a little clearer, but I still suffered from the shock, and I hardly realised what was happening.

I remember seeing Mr. Pickering and Mr. Bury lying on the ground as if asleep. I do not think they could have lived more than a few minutes in that awful atmosphere.

I staggered about in the thick darkness and tried to find my way out by wandering first in one direction and then another and suddenly I realised with horror that I was lost – utterly lost. I walked on and on until I came to a great fall. I was too exhausted to attempt to pass it and I collapsed.

Utterly Exhausted

After a minute or two it occurred to me that I might find a telephone. There are a large number scattered around the mine – about 30 I should think. I got up and eventually I found one and rang up the pit head again and again, but there was no reply. I realised that the telephone must have been damaged and I was plunged into despair.

I had not the slightest idea of my whereabouts and I reflected that it might be days before I was discovered. I sat down utterly exhausted and was trying to make up some plan of escape when I heard footsteps approaching. A moment later two rescuers came up to me. They dragged me to the pit bottom.

Perhaps some people might accuse me of cowardice for saving myself when all the others were killed but I could do nothing to help them and I think that anyone else would have acted as I did had they been in my circumstances.

Buried with a corpse

Another hairsbreadth escape was that which fell to the lot of Joseph Pearson, a middle age miner, who formed one of the ill-fated rescue party. Pearson was in the act of putting a corpse into a waggon when the second explosion occurred. He was thrown for several yards, and for some time lay insensible. When he came to himself he was upon the ground with the corpse beside him. Both he and the corpse were buried in the suffocating dust. Eventually he managed to struggle free and crawl to the pit bottom. He was badly cut about the body, but after treatment he was able to return home.

Well known local boxer as Ambulance man

"My heart's been bleeding all day long." Said Tommy Stokes, the well-known Mexborough boxer. Stokes, the hero of battles in London, Ireland, Scotland and Paris, to say nothing of his native town here, for 120 fights in all and has only lost 11, has a very tender heart and his voice was often husky as he told of scenes amongst the dying and the dead. For many hours on Tuesday he carried victims of the disaster from the pit head to the ambulance or the mortuary. He did the work of two men – did it literally, for the stretcher which he helped to carry went one man short all afternoon. It was a little tribute to his strength.

Before adopting the profession of a boxer, Stokes worked for several years in the mine and one of the corpses that he carried out on Tuesday evening was that of his old deputy. Among the dead is his cousin William Humphreys, the captain of the rescue party, who recently gave an exhibition before the King at Windsor

One man I helped to carry out suddenly began to moan, "Give me a drink! Give me a drink!" said the boxer. "I gave him a drink but he died before he could swallow it. Another man was still living, though insensible, had had the wooden parts of one of his clogs blown away and the nails were hammered right into his foot. I managed to wrench them out. Some of the sights I saw were too terrible for words."

King and Queen's visit Conisbrough
HISTORIC SCENES IN THE CASTLE GROUNDS

The day before the Disaster the King and Queen of England made an historic visit to Conisbrough Castle

KingGeorge V

Lining the route and crowding on the grassy slopes of the Castle grounds, there must have been 20,000 good and loyal citizens, actual and potential. For the children played an important part in the big demonstration of loyalty which greeted their Majesties during their progress from their entry into the village by way of the high road, overlooking the crags, to their arrival at the keep of the castle.

Seven Hundred Years Ago
It was a thrilling moment when the Castle caretaker, Richard Feirn, in response to a signal from the Castle gate ran up the Royal standard. Not for seven hundred years had that proud emblem denoting the presence of Royalty, floated over the grey pile. That was in the time of King John, though since that time the Castle has been in the possession of a British monarch, the warlike Edward the Fourth, and his younger brother, Richard of Gloucester, of detested memory, is said to have been cradled if not born there; while the ill omened Charles Stuart has occupied the Castle though not in majesty, but almost as a fugitive, listening to the sullen boom of Cromwell's guns as they battered the walls from the heights of Cadeby. Although the gaily bedecked crowds which awaited the coming of the King and Queen were not much occupied with meditation upon the grand history of the Castle of Kings (to give the literal interpretation of the word Conisborough), the appearance of the picturesque old ruin in the soft mellow light of the summer afternoon, the harshness of its grey walls gently broken with the plentiful verdure of its intermingling end supporting vinery, was one to draw forth general admiration, and certainly the Castle ground and the stately old keep had never looked as well as they did on Monday as they stood in-residence to receive yet another King. Those who had composed themselves on the slopes of the Castle yard received their intimation that the Royal party was at hand in the shape of a subdues roar from across the valley in the direction of the highroad from Doncaster and indistinctly through the trees could be discerned the gentle progress of 12 motor cars, through an avenue of agitated colour. Past the Star Hotel, and arrived at the steep declivity which takes the wayfarer off the highroad into the centre of the village, the first five cars detached themselves and the remainder went forward to Wentworth..

The Earl Unknown
In but a minute or two the Royal entourage had landed at the Castle Lodge, to the accompaniment of deafening cheering. Inside the Castle gates were assembled 3,600 children of the Conisborough and Denaby schools, in charge of their teachers, and their loyal outbursts must have been distinctly gratifying. At the castle gates, Mr.W.Lowry Cole C.C. agent to the Countess of Yarborough, owner of Conisborough' Castle, was presented by Earl Fitzwilliam to the King and Queen.

By the way, the Earl, who had looked in at the Castle grounds at three o'clock to see that all was in order, had a somewhat laughable experience, for on making his way to the holy of holies, the little enclosure of ground within the walls of the keep, where were the Royal pavilion and the provision tent, he was met with a sturdy refusal by a rustic Constable, who suspected him of being a Press man or something even worse. The Earl smiled, uttered the talisman "Fitzwilliam" and was allowed to proceed. "I didn't know who he was." muttered the conscientious but rather discomfited officer to a bystander. "Why didn't he wear a blooming badge?"

Rolling Cheers.
There could be no possibility of mistake this time. All eyes were eagerly centred on the leading pair in the little cortege up the shingle path to the gate of the keep. His Majesty, who was dressed in light grey and looked uncommonly well, extended his brown bowler hat in one continuous acknowledgement of the rolling cheers of the multitude and bowed from side to side as with dignified mien and measured step, he escorted his Queen to the Castle. Queen Mary bowed graciously in acknowledgment of the great reception accorded the Royal pair, and bestowed especial notice upon the children, who were ranged around almost at her feet. Behind the King and Queen came Mr. Lowry Cole, who at the invitation of the King, was to conduct the Royal party round the Castle, the King's private secretary, Lord Stamfordham. Earl Fitzwilliam, the Marquis and Marchioness of Zetland of the Countess Fitzwilliam, who were not of

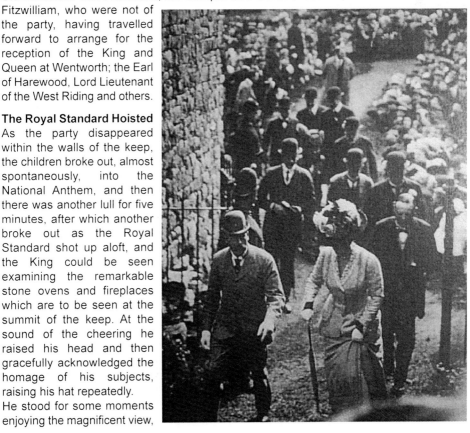

the party, having travelled forward to arrange for the reception of the King and Queen at Wentworth; the Earl of Harewood, Lord Lieutenant of the West Riding and others.

The Royal Standard Hoisted
As the party disappeared within the walls of the keep, the children broke out, almost spontaneously, into the National Anthem, and then there was another lull for five minutes, after which another broke out as the Royal Standard shot up aloft, and the King could be seen examining the remarkable stone ovens and fireplaces which are to be seen at the summit of the keep. At the sound of the cheering he raised his head and then gracefully acknowledged the homage of his subjects, raising his hat repeatedly. He stood for some moments enjoying the magnificent view,

which never looked better than it did yesterday afternoon, and he could be seen pointing out a special object of interest, which it transpired was the Priory, a Children's Convalescent Home, given by Mrs. Godfrey Walker to the Sheffield Royal Hospital, as a tribute to the memory of her husband.

The King displayed a good deal of interest in the old ruins. Unfortunately he was not accompanied by the Queen, who has not quite recovered from a recent injury and quickly tires with walking. Her Majesty went straight to the Royal pavilion, which consisted of a small but beautifully arranged and fitted tent, lined with ivory white martin and bedecked with fern. The tent had been sent down from Wentworth in the morning in charge of a. small party of butlers and footmen and tea was served at five tables in the pavilion.

A Rapid Survey.

Indeed, the stay in the castle did not occupy more than half-an-hour, the King making a rapid survey of the most interesting features of the keep, the dungeon, the oratory, the armoury, the fireplaces in which he was especially interest, and other objects off antiquarian interest. Mr Cole supplied the King with an epitomised history of the Castle and the King is said to have admired a good deal of what he saw.

He shook hands graciously with Mr. Cole as the Royal party left the Castle Grounds and then, to the accompaniment of much cheering, the Royal progress was resumed, through Hooton Roberts, Kilnhurst, Cabin Bar and the Haigh, to Wentworth. The police were splendidly organised and under the command of Mr. W. Quest, Deputy-Chief Constable of the Riding, Mr Johnson Hicks, Superintendent of the Doncaster West Riding Division and Inspector Barraclough and Ramsay, carried out their work quietly and effectively.

----

two days later the King and Queen visited Cadeby Main Colliery after the disaster

The King and Queen at the pit head

A visit to the colliery offices
Her Majesty's great grief

The visit of the King and Queen to the Cadeby mine on Tuesday evening brought comfort to the bereaved widows and mothers grouped along the roadside and at the approaches to the colliery. The King went to Cadeby fresh from his experience at Elsecar, where he had descended the Elsecar pit.

Earlier in the day the King had addressed a gracious message of sympathy to those concerned in the disaster. In the evening their Majesty's displayed in a practical manner the deep interest they are taking in the industrial life of their subjects by making a personal call at the offices of the of the Denaby and Cadeby colliery company, just before 7-30 o'clock. They drove to the front entrance of the officers in their motorcar, accompanied by Earl Fitzwilliam, Lord Stamfordham and Major Atcherley, Chief Constable of the West Riding.

It had been rumoured earlier in the day that a visit from their Majesty's might be expected , and when they arrived there was still a very large crowd present watching the sad operation of carrying out the dead bodies from the mine and quietly and reverently placing them in the temporary mortuary. As the Royal cars approached, all heads were bared, and their Majesty's alighted at the colliery entrance in absolute silence.

In the building the Royal party was received by Mr W.H.Chambers, the managing director of the company, and the Mr J.R.Wilson of Leeds, who was the only mines inspector to survive the second explosion, which entombed the rescue party. Both Mr Chambers and Mr Wilson were coal dust grimed and were wearing the clothes in which they had been down the pit.

Their Majesty's asked many pertinent questions about the disaster, and displayed a great interest in what the occurrence meant to the mining public. Plans showing the scene of the explosion were shown to their Majesty's and described by Mr Chambers, who explained the force of the explosion and the manner in which it expended itself by killing all who were in its path.

After a stay of about a quarter of an hour their Majesty's left the offices, their departure from Conisbrough being witnessed by the large crowd which had assembled. The King's features disclosed his great concern. It was as though he have suffered a great personal loss. As the Queen emerged with bowed head, tears still filled her eyes.

The presence of the King and Queen at such a moment and and their obvious sympathy with the sufferers had a remarkable effect on the spectators, many of whom, unable to restrain themselves by recollecting the terrible sights across the valley, involuntarily burst into cheers which, although somewhat misplaced, denoted their warm appreciation of their kindness which had prompted the King and Queen to visit the stricken village. Subsequently the following notice was issued from the colliery offices:

Their Majesties the King and Queen visited the Cadeby colliery today to ascertain personally on the spot all particulars of the sad calamity which has deprived many of those of those we love. They commanded me to express to all who have suffered loss of any who were dear to them, their deep sympathy with them in their grief
W.H.Chambers

The Queen and the Colliers widow
Gradually details are leaking out of the visit of the King and Queen to the offices at Denaby on Tuesday night. It has been freelly rumoured that the King expressed a desire to go down the mine to see the conditions existing there, but was persuaded by the colliery officials against the intention. No one however, attempts to confirm this, and at present it remains merely one of the best of legends rising on the lives of the imaginative.

But what is absolutely fact is that her Majesty the Queen betrayed the utmost concern at the grief of the widow of a collier who had come up to one of the enquiry offices to look at the list, and had found the name of her husband there. The poor woman was shrieking with distress when their Majesty's were descending the stairs. The officials made a dart to escort her Majesty clear of actual contact with this physical pain, but her Majesty turned aside and made enquiries as to the particular cause of the woman's lamentations.

When told of the cause she said the "Poor Poor thing!" and was proceeding to make furthering enquiries when Mr W.H.Chambers approached to escort her to his room, where the King was already eagerly gleaming particulars of the disaster. When their Majesty returned from the consultation with Mr Chambers and Mr Wilson, the Queen looked in the enquiry room and with tears in her eyes, asked the whereabouts of the bereaved woman whom she wished to see. But the woman had gone and the Queen had to depart without extending to her the sympathy and solace which it had been their intentions to bestow.

The Cadeby Disaster Inquest

Many Interesting Narratives
Graphic Stories of Second Explosion
Remarkable Escapes

Wednesday's proceedings

The jury was: Messrs H.H. Wray, J.T. Asher, William Isaac Gibbs, W.H. Appleyard, G. Appleyard, E.Dutton, G.Ellis, W.A.Lugar, A.Moody, J.Gillott, William Wilson and Edward Bell. The 12 good men and true appointed to serve on the jury charged with investigating the deaths of the 87 victims of the Cadeby colliery disaster on July 9, accomplished a great part of their duties on Wednesday, when they went into the subject matter of the inquest returned a verdict on the death of the 73 men whose bodies have been recovered. The inquest was held in the Denaby Main Hotel on Wednesday 24th July. . Mr Allen took his seat at 10.30 and amongst those present were the Home Office representative Mr. J.R.R. Wilson; Mr G. Poole, HM Inspector of mines, Mr W.H.Chambers, managing director of Denaby & Cadeby Collieries and Mr Herbert Smith, president of the Yorkshire Miners association.

How it was discovered

The South district was presented on the plan now before them. The explosion was first noticed by a road-layer named William Humphries, who said that between one and two in the morning he was going on with his work in the South district, when he noticed a stoppage in the air current and then a puff of return air in his face. Anyone who knew anything at all about mining would know that that would be indicative of an explosion, because the air-current was sent from the downcast shaft through all the workings to the upcast shaft, and they could quite see that this puff of air indicated that something was wrong with the ventilation, and that would indicate an explosion. Humphries communicated his suspicions to other workmen and shortly after they went round the whole of the workings and found, and found everybody within the scope of the explosion dead, and their bodies lying in the roads.

This was reported at the pit-bottom and at half-past-nine Mr. Pickering had arrived on the scene. Rescue parties were formed to deal with the emergency, and a large party of men went down. While they were in the workings a second explosion occurred, and brought down a large fall of roof which overwhelmed several of the men. Others were killed outright by the explosion or overcome by after-damp, and unfortunately the second explosion brought the death-roll up to eighty-seven, and we are told that there are now fourteen bodies in the mine. Steps were immediately taken to cut off the seat of the explosion, which was bound by the fourteens and thirty-threes levels, and brick stoppings were built. The first stopping was blown-out by a subsequent slight explosion, but it was rebuilt, and he was happy to say that the work of sealing up the area had gone on successfully, and that no further explosion had taken place, nor was any feared.

The Cause.

The actual cause of the disaster was at present unknown. It was supposed to have originated in a gob-fire, and the seat of that gob-fire was expected to be found near thirty-three's level. Gob-fires are common enough in South Yorkshire mines, and when they occurred they had to be dealt with. There were certain measures to be taken, and, in a large measure, they were taken successfully, but unfortunately on this occasion the reverse occurred. There were certain indications given. There was a heating and a smell, and explosive gasses were given off. After the gas was exploded, they got the after-damp, which consisted largely of the poisonous carbonic acid, and the men who were compelled to breathe it died. They had an instance of this in the case of Mr. Charles Bury, the manager of the mine, who was very badly 'gassed', and who subsequently succumbed to the effects of the carbonic acid.

The old man's narrative
Joseph Farmer, greaser, Denaby, said that about 1:40. he had a conversation with Humphries in the stable slip and Humphries told in that he had seen some dust, and the air current had reversed for a moment. Witness told him he thought it was an explosion this and he then went down the plane as far as 37's, where he found the greasers, which were always sawdusted, as black as ink with dust. He proceeded to 33's and went through 2 doors there to see if the ventilation was travelling down the return airway. Outside the second door the air was very foul and he shut the door and came back again. Coming to the point where the return air was carried over, he could hear it passing, and found everything as usual there. At 166's. He found the ventilation door all right, but also found lids and timber from the tubs blown away and collected about the road.

My God, there's no one alive!
He proceeded further until he found two or three tubs blown over the clips. Here his foot sank so deeply into the dust that he was a little alarmed and drew back for seven or eight yards, but then proceeded forward. The condition of the air here was good, and the first point at which he smelled anything of an explosion was at 33's doors, some hundred yards from 14's landing. It affected his head a little, and he returned to find Humphries. He shouted several times, but all was silent as the grave. When he got to the top of the plane, he met a man named Senior, who asked him what he had found. Witness replied, " My God, there is not a man alive down there !" The witness and Humphries went down the plane again, and when they got to the second door, there was Humphries, Nicholson, and Silvester come up from 33's. Witness set to them, "You're lucky you are alive!" After they examined the doors they proceeded in the direction of 14s level, walking in Indian file at intervals of 12 yards. At 14s level witness picked up some clips and a 5 inch bolt that had been blown off the rails. There was a 20 foot girder out, but there was not much muck down. He could not describe the position of the tubs. They were all piled up and smashed to pieces. It would be between three o'clock and four when they reached this point. Humphries, Bullock and he here they consulted agree that it would be wise to look over the top of the tubs. Eventually Bullock and Humphries went, while he remained there.

A Solitary Post
Cusworth and Springthorpe came up, and witness took their clothes and put them on one side. Springthorpe, said, "Stay here. Joe, while I come back." When Springthorpe returned, Cusworth was seated on a tub and he said to Springthorpe "How's the ventilation as regards a second explosion." Springthorpe's reply was that the current of air was working towards the men. Witness then told them that the 19's door was blown open and the Crossgate door was shut. Witness said that Mr Cusworth sent him to 33's is to prevent anyone from entering those doors. Springthorpe accompanied him, and when they got to 33's door Springthorpe wanted to go on further. The witness declined, saying, "No, I shall not go. I have had a fair turn. I have had my stomach turned. I will do anything to assist, but I will not go on there." Springthorpe went on a little way, then came back and told witness to stand at the doors and see that no one came through that way, but direct everybody to go down 14's. He drew

two empty tubs across the road, put a sleeper across them, marked "no road" in several places, and stood in the centre of the barrier to bar the progress of anyone who came that way. He thought it was wise.

Did William Humphries and Fisher afterwards come round to relieve you? – Yes, they came through and said there being right around the workings. Bullock said he had come across 22 dead bodies and five dead horses. I told them I was sorry. It was a sad tale to tell, and that I didn't think we should be needed as they were already 22 dead men accounted for and five horses, and the others, making the total to 31 must be at the far end. I stayed there until 8:10, and then we were relieved

South deputy broken down

The coroner announced that James Springthorpe, the deputy of the South district, who had lost a son in the second explosion, and had himself narrowly escaped, was too ill to appear and give evidence, and Mr Wilson had taken a statement from, which he (the coroner) would read aloud.

Mr Smith: Of course, I take it that he will come into the home office inquiry. He is one of the most important witnesses. The coroner: Oh, certainly

The statement was that James Springthorpe, resided at 143 Tickhill Street, was deputy in charge of the South district. He stated that he went down the pit at five o'clock on the morning of July 9th having heard that something was wrong. He went straight down the South plane, and was overtaken by Cusworth at 33 level end. Witness had an electric lamp as well as his own safety lamp. They saw Farmer lower down, and he said he did not think there was anyone alive. They could see what had happened. The tubs were tumbled about at 14's levels end. Humphries said, "I don't think anyone is living." Witness sent Humphries back to fetch Mr Bury and the rescue party. There were told that Fisher and Bullock had gone forward so Cusworth and he followed. On 14's they passed several bodies which were stiff and cold. They came across a closed-door at 19's Crossgate, and following footsteps in the dust, passed several bodies of men and horses. They went by 121's Crossgate the face at 19's. Getting back on 19 level. They sat down. Their heads were thumping. Witness asked what was knocking and found it was his own head.

The second explosion

They went on to 64's, and in sevens they found 3 dead bodies and three more in 64's. Some of the party went on but witness was getting bad. Mr Bury had found them at the bottom of the Crossgate, and went with them along 64's, 121's and 19's Mr Bury had sent a party round by the gate, and he, Murgatroyd, and witness went below 121's. Witness was stupefied. Mr Bury then sent him away as he was ill and went on himself. Murgatroyd brought witness out and he was given a drink by his (witnesses) son. Witness stayed at 14's level.

Littlewood was there, and a lot of men came, including three inspectors, conducted by Charles Prince, who was taking them to Mr Bury. Several bodies had gone by and witness and Littlewood were alone, when suddenly he heard a rush and a clap, and he said. "Look out, Herbert!" He was a 8 or 10 yards above the level, and his lamp was knocked flying. Charles Prince had gone by about 3 minutes when it happened. Eventually witness caught the rails and crawled. He saw a flame as well as the smoke and dust. There was such a rattle and clatter, but not much of a boom. Nicholson was just top side of it and they were feeling their way among the hot black dust. He got to 66's and met a lad who gave him a drink. Next, he met one at 33's. He was scorched, and his head smarted. Mr Basil Pickering helped him into the chair at the pit bottom. Mr Pickering knew that his father was down there. Witness's boy was at 19 Crossgate with Fred Horsfield. Mr Wilson divided the lamps amongst them as he met them coming up the gate. There were three gates in 19's Crossgate. The first was called the "smoke hole." There were two stoppings there and one in course of erection. In number two an electric lamp was burning when he went up there, and there was a stopping being built. In number three they were getting ready to build a stopping. No one was working in number three stopping and there was no stink there, though the three holes had a connection with an old fire. There was a stink in number two, and witness had been with Mr Bury there all the morning on Monday.

A Remarkable Escape
Percy Murgatroyd, filler, 42. Maltby Street, Denaby main, said he went to work at Cadeby on the morning of July 9 at six o'clock, and Humphries came to him and said, "Come on, you're wanted." He was a member of the rescue team and he went to the top at once and got his apparatus joining the rest of the team, and they set off immediately for the scene of the accident. They proceeded to 14's landing, which they found in a state of disorder. Tubs were smashed, falls were down, and girders were out. They proceeded to the bottom of 14's Crossgate, and a quarter of an hour later Mr Bury arrived. He accompanied Mr Bury on a round of inspection. Mr Bury said he would have one rescue man with his apparatus, not because he thought it would be wanted, but because there might be places which they could not get into without it. On 19 landings they came to a wall partly built, and there were appearances that it had been left in a hurry. An electric lamp was burning, was not damaged, but a safety lamp near had been put out. In 64's they found four bodies, but he only knew one of them, and that was Charlie Fletcher. He noticed that the props were scorched and had about an eighth of an inch of coal dust. They gave no indication of the way the explosion had travelled, for they were scarred all round. The coal face was more like a stone face. Mr Bury made an examination of all the places they went into, and found things in practically the same condition. They proceeded along to 121's, Mr Bury making observations all the time. At 121's they found the temperature very high, the air current was practically normal.in 19's Crossgate they met Mr Douglas Chambers, who wished to accompany Mr Bury round all of the affected area – witness supposed in order to see if they could come to any conclusion as regarding the cause of the accident. In 64's they found a watch hanging hard by a body and it was stopped at 1:30. When they were in sevens old gate he remembered that Mr Douglas Chambers through a handful of dust in the air to test the current, and, though he followed it with a powerful electric lamp, he could find no motion whatever. It was practically stagnant. Mr Bury and Mr Chambers remained in 19's and consulted for a few minutes. They were not quite sure under which of two falls a certain body unaccounted for, was located. Whilst the falls were being cleared away, Mr Pickering came up with the two other inspectors, and that would be between our past 10 and 11 o'clock.

Havoc amongst the officials
They consulted for a minute or two, and stood on one side to let a stretcher party pass with a body. Witness was with Mr Bury, Mr Pickering, Mr Douglas Chambers, Mr Hewitt and Mr Tickle. He had his apparatus on, and that was what saved him from what followed.
The coroner: Just describe the second explosion.
Murgatroyd: Those who work in a pit will know what the sound of a door being closed with a lot of air pressure behind it is like. The first shock was similar to that, but the roar which followed was like the blasting at a powder works. It kept up a continuous roaring. The ventilation was stopped for a time, but I saw no flame. The gate got full of dust and smoke and afterdamp, and in a short time. It was so thick that, though I held my electric lamp straight in front of my face, I could only just see it. After it happened, Mr Bury and the others knew in a minute what it was, and Mr Douglas Chambers and Mr Bury and others shouted,

"down on your faces, lads, keep cool," or something like that, and we all went down.

The coroner: and how long do you think it was before you were able to move? – Not so very long, I am sure, because as soon as I was able I had my tubes in my mouth. It could not have been long, because if I had not been quick in getting them in, I should not have been here.

Continuing witness said that after the blast and passed, and he got the tubes in his mouth, he got up and went in the direction of the Crossgate, which was the wrong way, and ran up against a girder, which pulled him up. His apparatus was working very satisfactory, and he turned in the other direction toward the door, which he reached after crossing two small falls. He could not tell what was the condition of the atmosphere, for he had lost his goggles, and was covering his face with his hand. In 14's landing he stumbled over some bodies, and he was so weak he could not rise for 10 minutes to go on. There were bodies all the way, and he met with a very large fall at the junction. He could not get over it so he rang to the pit bottom from a telephone which was near and then lay down, and knew no more until someone came and told him that he did not need his apparatus, and that the air was quite good. He then took out the tubes and put them into the mouth of a man lying near, but without effect. He met Mr Witty about 200 yards beyond the four, and told him where Mr Pickering, Mr Bury, Mr Chambers and the rest were lying.

A journey among the dead

After a short interval for lunch Benjamin J Hadfield was called, and said he was a deputy at Denaby Main and residing at 115 Tickhill Street, Denaby. He was returning from work at 6:25 on the morning of July 9 when he was informed that there have been an accident at Cadeby, and he proceeded to the colliery in order to take part in the rescue work if required. He met Mr Witty there, and was told by him that he had telephoned to Sergeant Winch and had received a message from the pit that 22 bodies had been located and that the ventilation had been restored. Witness waited for Sgt Winch, who arrive shortly after seven o'clock with apparatus. Sgt Winch proceeded to the offices for orders, and during his absence, the other Denaby rescue men, Ward, Summerscales and Lawrence arrived, and they all descended the pit and proceeded down the South plane. They reached 14's level about eight o'clock, and found seven bodies on the road. At 14 they met the first rescue party under Harry Hully, who told them that they have made a thorough inspection of the district, understood that there was no fire. The Denaby party were proceeding towards the face to help with anything that they were required to do. They met Mr Bury and reported themselves to him. He told them there was no need for the rescue apparatus, as the ventilation had been restored. He was asked about fire, and he said there was no fire from the explosion. He told them not to interfere with three bodies near a stopping, because he wanted the inspectors see them, they look so peculiar, and their attitude suggested that they had been running away from their work places. He told them to reserve their electric lamps for fear they would need them.

A Ghastly Inspection

They proceeded under the leadership of Mr H Williamson to the bottom of 19's cross gates, where they fell Fred Horsfield, who was taking notes of the dead bodies. They also found another party, including Cusworth, and they had a dead body there waiting for the stretcher party. Their party went forward into 121's where they found the dead body of a horse which had apparently been killed while in the act of turning round towards its tub. Just behind the tub they came across two dead bodies. One appeared as if he had been killed as he was having his snap, fully was seated with a bottle in one and his basket across his knees. There was another body near. It was laid on its right side, and both bodies were slightly burned. After removing the bodies they proceeded into 14 gate, and there they found

Richardson's stick and lamp. They found nothing in 14's stall and turned into 153's. There they found two safety lamps on the ground, extinguished, but otherwise unharmed, and they marked the position of these lamps on the roof. At 131's turning they found a body lying with its heels towards the face having apparently been blown forward. Just by the turning they found the body of another man. He was lying with his head towards the stall, the opposite way to the other man. They moved 2 tubs at 121 junction to allow a passage for the stretcher parties, and here they also found a body seated astride a box. Going forward to the face they found three bodies together. One was burnt slightly, the other 2 showed no mark at any kind, but the third was burnt frightfully and he returneded with the stretcher party for this one, for he did not want them to see the body as he thought it would upset them. He left Williamson, Humphreys, Cusworth and Jackson behind in the store. There was still one body left there, and two watches were found hanging near. The one was stopped at 6.30 and the other at 1.30. At 19 junction there were stretcher parties with several dead bodies. They met first. Ellis and Evans and then Mr Pickering, Mr Tickell and Mr Hewitt were being conducted by Charles Prince, and later by Mr Wilson and Mr Hudspeth. The report itself to Mr witty and told him with the exception of a few the bodies are being located. He then left the pit having been on all night.

The Agent's Story
Harry Sykes Witty, of Denaby main, agent to the Denaby and Cadeby collieries, said he was at home when he received intimation, by a telephone message of the accident. He got into communication with the pit, and then got in touch on the telephone with Mr Pickering at Doncaster, and also with the Wath rescue station. After that he proceeded to the pit head, and found that Mr Bury, Mr Cusworth and the rescue parties had gone down the pit. By this time a large crowd had assembled at the bridge, and the police had arrived. He made arrangements to receive the bodies, and had the pay shed converted to this purpose, with Josiah Westby in charge. He sent her all the stretches from head quarters, about 20 in number. He had a message from the pit bottom that 22 bodies had been located, that the ventilation had been restored and that the rescue parties were going round the workings without apparatus. The message also said that a lot of men and stretches were required to remove the bodies. Mr WH Chambers was not at home at the time, and witness Telegraphed him. Mr Douglas Chambers, the manager of the Denaby Main mine, arrived at Cadeby about seven o'clock. Mr Hewitt was the first of the inspectors to arrive, and Mr Pickering and Mr Tickle came about 9:30. Mr J.P. Chambers, the managing director of the Cottonwood colliery and Mr G.H.Ashwin, agent of Wath main colliery, also arrived early. Before Mr Pickering descended the mine witness asked him whether he wished him (witness) to go within. He said, please yourself but I think you had better remain here.

Where the officials died
Proceeding to describe the spot where Mr Pickering's party met their fate, Mr Witty said. "Mr Bury was lying with his leg is under Mr Hewitt's head, and there were two other men on top of him. He was bleeding and so was Farmer, and they were the only two that any signs of life in their. I pulled them out into the fresh air"
The coroner: Did the atmosphere produce any impression on you? – Yes, it made my head thump a bit
When you had pulled Mr Bury and Farmer out of the fresh air did you return? – Yes
Sergeant Winch came and I directed him to go with the stretcher party. When I was proceeding to the 14's and 19's, I thought there was one among a group of bodies which showed some signs of life. I heard one breathing, but I could not tell which it was, though I felt them all. When I came back the breathing had ceased.

On Mr Chamber's arrival did you return to the mine with him? – Yes

After consultation were orders given to cut off the affected area with brick stoppings? – Yes

Was that done? – Yes

Witness, continuing, said that about three o'clock on the following morning he had information that another explosion had occurred and that the brick stoppings have been blown down. He went down the plane and examined the place, taking with him some men, who rebuilt the stoppings and proceeded to increase the thickness by putting up further walls, and now the thickness of one of the stoppings was 15 feet and of the others 9 feet. They had since been watched at intervals and had been found to serve their purpose.

The Surviving Inspectors

The last chapter in the connected story promised at the outset by the Coroner was supplied by Mr. John R. Robert Wilson, of Leeds, Senior Inspector of Mines, who gave his evidence in the form of a report.

He stated that at about seven-thirty on the morning of the 9th of July he was called upon the telephone by Mr. Pickering, who informed him that he had been trying to get in touch with him since half-past-six, and told him that there had been an explosion at the Cadeby Colliery, and that he was afraid a few men had been killed. He explained that he had to meet his Majesty the King at ten o'clock that morning and he was anxious that he (witness) should go and ascertain what had happened. He said he had telephoned Mr. Hewitt, who would probably get there before witness. He took with him Mr. Hudspeth and when they reached Cadeby they learned the magnitude of the disaster, and that not only had Mr. Hewitt arrived, but Mr. Pickering and Mr. Tickle, and that they had gone across to the colliery. When Mr. Hudspeth and he got across they found that their colleagues had just gone down. Mr. Witty explained to him that all the men on thirty-three's and fourteen's had been killed, that the district had been completely examined and that no gas or fire was now to be found. Mr. Basil Pickering, manager of Wath Main, who knew the district well, offered to conduct them, and Mr. G.H. Ashwin asked to be allowed to go in the party, and he was invited to do so. They went down at eleven o'clock.

A Graphic Story By The Inspector

They waited, continuing the inspector, at the South plane, to take off their clothes, and were proceeding toward 14 level when they were met by a sudden blast of slightly warm air, and they turned and ran. They had only gone a few yards, however, when witness noticed that the air current had resumed its normal course, and he called a halt. One or two men joined them in the darkness, some of them suffering from burns and bruises, and witness apportioned the lamps among the combined company, and they made for the level once more. At 14's level. Their encountered a huge fall of roof which blocked the roadway, and going through the second door encountered smoke and after damp. They sent to the pit bottom for assistance and settle down to wait, but searching about, Mr Hudspeth, who had an electric lamp, found he could squeeze between a falling girder and the wheels of an overturned tub. They heard a faint voice at the other side. It was Murgatroyd who was saying that he did not know what the air was like. He was wearing an apparatus and he was too weak to get through the fall. Witnesses lamp was behaving strangely, and there was gas on top of the fall. Mr Hudspeth got through and assisted witness to get through, and then they assured Murgatroyd that he was quite safe as the air was good.

Mr Chambers finds his son

Then they came across a group of nine bodies, only two of which were alive. A little further, they found 23 bodies. Mr J.E.Chambers and another man came up and Mr Chambers asked witness to follow him and keep his light in sight. He did so for a while, but he lost Mr Chambers and got to 19 crossgate. In the bend of the crossgate a man was lying badly injured, but alive.

As witnesses eyes were smarting and his head throbbing he returned to enquire for Mr Chambers. Mr Chambers returned shortly afterwards, having found his son, and witness persuaded him to go out of the pit. He also came across Mr Witty, who informed him that he had found prop burning. Mr Witty went forward and found the bodies of the three inspectors and the managers near the top of the 19 landing. Witness went up the crossgate and watched the effect of the pulmoters on one or two of the men until the rescue party arrived and reported that there was no fire.

Connected Chain Of Narrative

The coroner said the inquiry would terminate here for the present. They had ample evidence to assist in finding out how the men died, and also sufficient evidence to enable them to come to a conclusion as to by what means they died. It was not within the province of the jury to go further than that. They had heard the eight witnesses. Their memory was probably quite as good as his own, and they were not likely to forget for many years to come, the story of the Cadeby disaster. Then endeavoured to give a connected chain of narrative, leading from the first explosion, which was terrible enough, to the second, which was much more serious in its consequences. He did not think there ever had been an explosion which had involved the death of so many highly placed officials. All human life was valuable, but the very fact that three inspectors, to managers, and a number of deputies, had been taken from them and rendered it rather more difficult to present the story to them than it otherwise would have been. He thought they ought not to attempt to express an opinion as to the cause of the disaster.

Mr Smith Scarcely Satisfied

The jury retired and consulted for 20 minutes, and then the end of which they returned, and Mr H.H. Wray, the foreman announced that they returned a verdict of "accidental death, caused by two gas explosions in the Cadeby colliery on July 9, 1912."
Mr Smith. "Is that all the finding of the jury?"
The Coroner (surprise): "yes, that is all. You don't suggest that it is murder do you?"
Mr Smith: but isn't something to be said about the people were prevented from making inquiries? The Coroner:" I think it is a very proper verdict
The foreman: "We have tried to keep clear of any future inquiry that may be made"
The Coroner "they don't say that anyone is either to blame or is not to blame"

Gratitude To The Jury.

The coroner said that before the present inquest was closed. (There would have to be another on the remaining 14 victims).he must thank the jury for the services they had rendered, not only to the West riding, but to the inhabitants of their own district. They had all cheerfully assisted him night and day for the purpose of expeditiously dealing with bodies that were brought to the surface to avoid any delay in identification; but, further than that he believed all of them had rendered valuable assistance to the relatives and friends of the dead. They were there at the pit top, doing what they could, and performing the last offices for the dead, and if the county at large new the splendid nature of the work they had done, they would heartily support what he had to say on that subject. When he realised that it was all done outside their ordinary duties, and to mitigate the horror of the disaster, they would all agree that a few words he had spoken were well merited, for the performance of duty well done carried its own reward. He did not think there was need to say more at this point

DEBATE IN THE HOUSE OF COMMONS
July 5th 1913

Weakness of Mine's Act Admitted
Mr Fred Hall's Allegations.
A Motion Withdrawn.

The Cadeby main disaster of July last formed the subject of severe comment during the course of a remarkable parliamentary debate in the House of Commons on Wednesday, and the conduct of the Denaby and Cadeby Collieries Ltd, together with that, of the managing director, Mr W H Chambers was exposed to strong criticism. As a result of the debate the Home Secretary foreshadowed a considerable amendment of mining legislation

HOME SECRETARY AND THE RESPONSIBILITY.

During question time Mr Wadsworth (Labour, Hallamshire) asked the Home Secretary whether he had received a copy from the Miners Federation of Great Britain of Mrs Smiley and Hartshorne's report of the enquiry held into the Cadeby main colliery disaster of July 9 last year, in which they allege there were breaches of the Coal Mines Act; whether he was satisfied that such breaches of the Coal Mines Act did take place and, if so, whether it was his intention to take any action against the management at this colliery.

Mr McKenna: I have received a copy of this report from the Miners Federation. As regards the two points on which the report alleges breaches of the Act, the chief inspector, as a result of his enquiry, came to the conclusion that the requirements of the act had not been complied with on these points, but he formed the opinion that the responsibility laid primarily with the manager, who lost his life, and that in the circumstances set out in his report and, and, in view of the fact that the fire would in all probability have been got under without accident had the directions of the managing director being carried out, proceedings could not be taken with any prospect of success against the managing director. I have addressed a letter to this effect to the Miners Federation. The report of Mr Smiley and Mr Hartshorne was not forwarded by the Miners Federation to the Home Office until May 30th, whereas the time allotted by the Act for the institution of proceedings had expired in January.

MR CHAMBERS, NOT THE MANAGER.

Mr Brace (Labour Glamorgan South) asked whether the right honourable gentleman was aware that at the enquiry presided over by Mr Redmayne, Chief Inspector of Mines, into the cause of the explosion, by which 80 lives were lost, Mr Chambers, managing director of the company, declared he would not under similar circumstances withdraw the workmen from the mine, despite the fact that it was a grave violation of the coal mines regulation not to do so; and whether, in the face of such a declaration, in which he wholly failed to realise his responsibility for human life, the right honourable gentleman considered Mr Chambers was a fit and proper person to have miners lives placed under his care?

Mr McKenna: I do not think it possible for me to argue the case. In answer to a question I have consulted Mr Redmayne on this point, and I am informed by him there is no power under the Act to proceed. If there is a case against the managing director, there would be power under section 11 of the act of 1911 to institute enquiry into the competency of the holder of a certificate, if the holder is performing the duties of manager. But Mr Chambers did not perform the duties of manager, but managing director of the company. As Managing Director you would not be liable to any proceedings. The manager there was killed. Consequently, both on the ground of time and personal responsibility, there is no possibility of action being taken.

Mr Brace intimated that as the reply was not satisfactorily, and the matter was of vital importance, the board move the adjournment of the house to call attention to it.

HISTORY OF THE DISASTER

At 8.15 in accordance with notice given, Mr Brace moved the adjournment of the house in order, he said, to discuss the matter of great public importance. The number of lives destroyed every year by mining equal roughly, the number of lives lost by the Titanic, and anything that added to the danger of so dangerous an industry demanded that the Home Office as the administrative authority should use all its resources to make mining less dangerous. He called attention to this matter on behalf of the Miners Federation of Great Britain, who felt themselves very aggrieved with the circumstances involved in connection with the Cadeby Main colliery explosion, which occurred on July 9, 1912. The colliery gave employment to nearly 1000 men on the day shift and 505 on the night shift, and they were faced with the peculiar situation that in the person of Mr W.H. Chambers they had a general manager, who took a very active part in the management of the colliery. Mr Redmayne's report showed that Mr Chambers accepted the responsibility of giving the orders, and if that were so, he must accept the responsibility for the result. It was because they felt that they were faced with a situation in which a dead colliery manager was being made to carry the burden of responsibility for the disaster that they raised the matter in the House, in order to put an end to the situation which was dangerous to the lives and limbs of their people. The miner's delegates Mr Smiley and Mr Hartshorne ascertained that the first gob fire at Cadeby occurred about 1906 or 1907, when no life was lost. A second broke out at a subsequent date. There was a third gob fire in November 1911, with which the management wrestled until April 1912. On January 20, 1912 an explosion occurred in the locality of the July explosion, and four men were slightly burned, and the whole of the men in the district came out, being very much frightened.

A LIVE GASOMETER.

It was apparent from these and other circumstances recorded in the report that the house was dealing with a mine, which was nothing more less than a live gasometer (Labour cheers) and well within the knowledge of the manager. The temperature at the face was 94°, in the air current 90° and on the intake 80°. The two explosions on July 9, 1912, resulted in the loss of 88 lives. He had never read a record that impressed him more of the danger of a mine (Labour cheers). The condition of affairs was very difficult to understand. For some reason best known to themselves, the workmen seemed to have kept silent upon the condition of the mine. The evidence at the enquiry showed that the afterdamp and the gas was so terrific that after working only 2 to 4 min men became unconscious. The conditions were such as to teach any management that there were face-to-face with a situation which, on their honour and in their solemn obligation to the men, they ought not to allow the men to go into. (Cheers) It was a wilful disregard of responsibility. (Cheers) Their dispute with the Home Office was that they were unable to bring home the responsibility tp the right quarter. Mr Chambers, who, after all, was the responsible man, said at the enquiry that he gave certain orders to the manager, who was dead and that had those orders been carried out there would have been no danger. The time had now come whether other than verbal orders should be given to an official. (Cheers) He (Mr Brace,) submitted to the House that no manager or official, had he been given an order to carry out a particular piece of work in a particular way would have dared venture not to carry out that instruction. They could not accept Mr Chambers evidence, and they made the serious charge that due precaution was not taken to protect the lives and limbs of the men in consequences of the very bad conditions they found the men in. What was more, despite this condition of the mine, no word was sent to the Mines inspector, Mr Pickering, who gave his life to solve the problem of the fire.

MINERS LIVES SHOULD BE HELD SACRED.

The honourable member quoted innumerable extracts from the evidence given during the enquiry into the disaster bearing on irregularities and asked what was the Home office going to do in the matter? Were they going to stand idly by and allow the management to shelter themselves besides some kind of technicality, although they were violating the Coal Mines Regulation Act, which the house passed for the better protection of the lives and limbs of the miners? The record of the conditions existing in the mine prior to disaster ought to have been sufficient to teach any management that they were sending these men to their deaths unless they were protected by the providence of God. By every rule of the size of mining explosion was a natural result of the condition of affairs which was reported to have existed at the mine. In many mines throughout the country this kind of thing was going on at the present moment, and humanity demanded that for a moment they should stop in their ordinary legislative work to lay down the conditions that miners lives should be held sacred. (Hear, hear). There was a callousness about this accident which absolutely appalled him. While 35 bodies were lying in the pit the day shift came in, lower down the shaft without knowing of this terrible disaster. In Wales if there was disaster of half the damage, the people would have known of it and been on the spot. In the other pit the men continued working in the ignorance of what could happen and some hundreds of tonnes of coal were raised. Only when the inspectors arrived was winding of coal put an end to.

A RECENT INCIDENT.

Mr F Hall (Labour Normanton) in seconding in the motion, said for many years past there was not a man employed in this particular colliery who dared lodge a complaint against anything that was done by the management for fear of dismissal. (Cries of shame) An attempt had been made to put all of the responsibility upon the man who unfortunately was dead but the agent of the colliery was still living. The man who acted as agent at the time of the disaster was not the agent today. He did not know whether the Home Office had taken any step with regard to cancelling this man's certificate. The man who was agent at that time was now deputy at the same colliery, but he was, it was said, been paid exactly the same salary as when he was agent. If that were so, the reducing of the man was only a farce, and was done for the purpose of keeping him outside any prosecution. The under manager was still living, and he had been driven from pillar to post. He was a miner who had risen from the rank of work man. No doubt there was some responsibility upon him, but his certificate had been taken away. Last Monday, he (Mr Hall) had to go down to Yorkshire because of another accident at the colliery, and while it was there he was informed that there was nearly a riot in that very village on Monday night last. The reason for that was that a fatal accident had occurred through a large fall of earth in the roadway and a man was killed, and was lying there, and the company endeavoured to force the whole of the men of another shift to walk over the dead body. (Cries of shame). He as one of the representatives of the Yorkshire Miners Association as well as his a honourable friend who represented the Miners Federation of Great Britain, desired to know what action the Home Secretary proposed to take to see that an end was put to the tyranny practised at these particular collieries which is more than at any others in the county which he had belonged. (Labour cheers).

HOME SECRETARY'S STATEMENT.

Mr McKenna said the Home Office had always shown itself more desirous to secure the safety of the miners than he could well express in words. What had been said had not disclosed any blameable action or neglect on the part of the Home Office. He would not wish to defend his office merely on that account. The accident at Cadeby mine occurred in July last year. The circumstances which preceded the accident were exactly as described by his honourable friends. Gobfire was discovered in the mine four days before the accident occurred. That was a condition which everybody in the mine knew was indicative of serious danger. It appeared upon the evidence that the managing director of the mine, when the gobfire was discovered, he gave orders that all the passages to the locus of the fire should be built up. There was no evidence at the enquiry to rebut the statement made by Mr Chambers. It was undoubted that an examination of the mine showed that one of the passages to the locus of the fire was not built up. The result of that was that air could penetrate into the region which had been described as a live gasometer. Two explosions took place and 88 lives were lost. All those facts were undisputed. Who was to blame? There being undoubted breach of the Act of 1911. It had been said that no notice was sent by the management to Mr Pickering, the inspector employed by the Home Office. If he had received notice no doubt he would have acted but neither the Home Office nor their agent got notice of the facts. His honourable friends had said that notice should be given by Mr Chambers but the Act said notice ought to be given by the manager. The manager was dead. His honourable friends said that this was one of the cases where all the blame was put on someone who was dead and the man over him got off scot free. The charge against the Home Office was not that they were directly to blame for the accident, but that when the breaches of the act came to their knowledge they did not prosecute Mr Chambers. Mr Chambers was not the manager. The manager was killed in the accident and the fault was his. The next charge was that there was no evidence that Mr Chambers gave the order that all the passages the gob fire should be built. It was true that there was no evidence except Mr Chambers's evidence. Then it must be remembered that no proceedings could be taken against Mr Chambers, or anyone else except within six months of the accident. The last month expired last January and the Home office had no grounds for proceeding against Mr Chambers before January 1913.

LEGISLATION PROMISED

The accident had disclosed three serious defects in the existing law. The Mines act was passed no later than 1911, but such was the variety of the conditions under which mining was carried on, such were its dangers, that, however great the experience of the Department might be, and whatever precautions might be taken, subsequent experience showed that the new amendment of the law was required. In the first place no action could be taken except within a period of six months after the accident, taking place. There were certain exceptions and, they did not arise in this case. What did that mean in a case like this? The accident occurred in the beginning of July 1912. It was one of the conditions of the continuance of the mine that the locus of the accident should be dammed off. Attempts are being made again and again to inspect the place where the accident occurred, but it had been found impossible to inspect the actual place. An enquiry was held immediately after, but months went by, and necessarily went by before the facts could be known. With all possible expedition, the evidence in this case was not completed until the beginning of December, five months after the accident. Report was not in draft until the end of January, more than six months after the accident had taken place. He readily admitted to his honourable friend that if a prima facie case had been disclosed in any part of the evidence on which a prosecution could have succeeded against Mr Chambers, or anyone else, an interim report would have been issued in order that proceedings might be begun within the period laid down in the Act. There was no such evidence. Before the report was completed six months had expired, and the question then became one of Platonic interests. He proposed at the earliest opportunity to introduce an amendment of the Coal Mines Act extending the period during which a prosecution may be begun to three months after the enquiry the accident had been completed. The second effect arose being the construction of clause 11 layout which provided that the Secretary of State might order an enquiry to be held with a view to determining who was in default, but it did not provide for suspending the certificate Labour superior to the manager.

HOME SECRETARY AND MR CHAMBERS.
He gathered from the speech of his honourable friend that he conceived they might have proceeded to hold an enquiry with a view to suspending Mr Chamber's certificate. He would certainly go through the evidence most carefully in view of what had been stated, that Mr Chambers had acted in the capacity of manager. Technically he was not the manager of the mine, but the managing director. But he would lay that evidence and statements of his honourable friends before the law officers of the Crown and if they advised him that his honourable friend's statement would bear the interpretation which he had put upon them, he should be most happy to order an enquiry under section 11. He had not yet not done so because he considered that the evidence was not such as would justify holding Mr Chambers liable as manager, but there was a defect in the Act as it stood, and the law should be so amended that a person superior to the manager, when he was really in truth the manager, must be liable to have his certificate suspended just as if he was the manager himself. The third defect was that while Section 67 laid down the requirements for the withdrawal of the men in case of danger in general terms, it left it open as a matter of opinion whether such circumstance has existed some days prior to the accident did, in fact, constitute, a dangerous condition within the meaning of the clause. He was advised that should a condition of things ought not to be made a matter of opinion, and he was asking the committee , which had been appointed to consider the whole subject to report to him at once on this limited branch of their enquiry with a view to the immediate issue of regulations. His technical advisers strongly recommended such regulations as will provide that the men ought to be withdrawn in all cases similar to those existing at the Cadeby mine prior to the accident. After the explanation he had given he hoped his honourable friend would not think it necessary to press his motion.

A CHAMPION FOR MR CHAMBERS.
Sir A.B.Markham (Labour Mansfield) said he very much regretted that this question have been brought before the house. He had no interest in the Cadeby colliery, although he was a managing director of an adjoining mine. He very much regretted that Mr Brace used his position in that House to make statements reflecting on men who were not there to defend themselves. Mr Chambers was the last man in the world not to accept responsibility for all orders he gave. He was the greatest authority in the country, probably on gob fires, and if there was a violation of the Act, the honourable member (Mr Brace) was perfectly able through his association to institute, a prosecution, and have all the facts brought out in a court of law.

Mr Brace: no one knows better than the right honourable Baronet that the employee has no right to take action against employers, although the employers have rights to take action against the workmen.

PANIC IN THE MINE.
Owing to the researches, largely of the mining Institute, he believed we were within measurable distance of making it impossible to have any great coal mine explosions in the future. He could not believe that the managers of the mine had shown callous disregard of

human life. He could not conceive that any human being could be so brutal as deliberately to allow men to go into a mine after an explosion had occurred. He knew, although he was unable to produce evidence, that no one knew at the time these men were let down that an explosion had taken place. As a matter of fact, what happened was that everyone lost their heads. It was just as well the house should know that – there was a panic in the mine. Under the terrible conditions followed a mine explosion, it was not easy to keep a calm judgement. As far as the mines with which he was connected were concerned the officials of the men's union might go down. There was nothing to conceal. Still – unwisely, he thought – the Cadeby officials had taken a different view. The statements made by Mr Brace were highly coloured. He admitted, however, there was danger, and it was what they had to fight against. He said most deliberately, that there was not a single mine today in Great Britain that was worked in conformity with the Mines Act. He believed there were something like 1000 regulations of one sort and another and the House went on adding to these intricate regulations and orders. It was impossible that every single detail in these orders could be attended to. After all, the manager was only really a human being, and in some mines they were 30 miles of road. If Mr Brace could point out how lives could be saved, he would have the support of the mining world, and the committee would welcome any evidence he might give or any suggestion he could make to them.

GREAT DIFFICULTIES.

Mr Meysey–Thompson (Conservative Handsworth) said he had a large number of miners in his constituency, and for many years yet much concern to find a means of preventing these accidents, and when, unfortunately, they occurred of minimising the loss of life. That debate had thrown a good deal of light on the cause of accidents, and had brought out some valuable suggestions. There were great difficulties owing to the varying circumstances under which accidents occurred and it was impossible to foresee in every case what ought to be done. He urged that the provision of life-saving apparatus should be compulsory in every district. He felt that these men ought not to be called upon to work under dangerous condition, and in this case he thought the conditions were distinctly dangerous. They were told over and over again that machinery existed for dealing with these accidents, when they occurred; it was found over and over again that they were not dealt with in a satisfactory manner by the Home Office. He sympathises with honourable members and will raise this discussion which might result in the Home Office taking proper precautions in the future.

SOLD ONCE MORE.

Mr Brace said that accepting the declaration of the Home Secretary at its full face value, he asked leave to withdraw the motion. Leave to withdraw was refused by several Unionist members, and the debate continued.

Mr Norman Craig (Conservative Thanet) expressed the hope that the Home Secretary before he too obligingly and complacently accepted the suggestions made, would consider very carefully the question of gob fires and the effect of withdrawing the men, because if a gob fire in a particular place was after withdrawal, as most men of science, said, going to create gob fires all the mine, then withdrawal was not merely closing the mine to the fire, but to the workers and creating difficulties in a very great number of directions.

Mr McKenna at 9.55 moved that the question be now put. The Speaker accepted the motion, and the opposition challenged a division, but the closure was carried by 262 votes to 143. The motion for adjournment was then negatived without a division, amid prolonged opposition ironical Cheers and Labour cries of "Sold once more."

Heroes Honoured

Mexborough Times August 16th 1913.

Presented to the King.
Edward medals be stored.
Royal recognition of splendid bravery.

The great Cadeby colliery disaster of July 9, 1912, has been prolific in its unpleasant after-effects, but it had at least one consequence which was gratifying and pleasurable – that of the declaration by the King of six of the gallant fellows who risked their lives so willingly and cheerfully in the flaming and poisoned mine on that and many succeeding days.

The announcement made some months ago that a batch of Edward medals was to be awarded in connection with the rescue work, which was carried out at Cadeby was the subject of general approbation, the only matter for regret being that the supply of medal was limited, and hopelessly unequal to the number of gallant fellows who were worthy to wear them. The decision to award the Victoria cross of the mine to this brave half-dozen was shortly followed by the announcement that a number of other courageous rescue workers were to be similarly honoured at the hands of the hospital order of St John of Jerusalem.

The names of those who on Tuesday morning attained the supreme distinction of decoration by Royal hands are:

Harold Hulley, Assistant Underground Manager at the Cadeby colliery, of Tickhill Square, Denaby main.
George Fisher, Deputy, Tickhill Square, Denaby main.
These men were awarded the Edward medal of the first-class (Silver)
The remaining four, will receive the Edward medal of the second class (Bronze):
J Edwin Chambers, General Manager of the Cortonwood Collieries, Brampton Bierlow
Herbert Williamson, Electrical Engineer at Cadeby colliery, of Conisbrough.
Walter Prince, Colliery Contractor, at Cadeby of the Glen Mexborough
PC Winch, Rescue Instructor of the Wath colliery rescue station

HOW THE MEDALS WERE EARNED

George Fisher

The majority of our readers will be familiar with the splendid coolness and courage which distinguished these men in a time of dreadful confusion and terrifying uncertainty, but for the benefit of those who are not, the merits of their conduct may be briefly explained.

Hulley and Fisher (the former, has since been promoted) were at the time both deputies in districts other than the fatal South, and they were among the earliest arrivals on the scene of the explosion. Indeed, Fisher was the first official to enter the exploded district on that fateful morning, having been summoned thither by a road man named Humphreys, who first made the discovery that something was wrong.

Fisher made a complete tour of the district, taking observations

Harry Hulley

Herbert Williamson

Walter Prince

throughout, and his evidence, was of considerable value to the Home Office enquiry. His was an experience calculated to try an iron nerve, and he displayed high courage in undertaking so terrible a tour of inspection.

Later, Harry Hulley, who had brought a rescue team down the pit, made the same tour in company with the ill-fated Mr. Charles Bury, the manager of the mine. Both these men have been working all night, and were sent out of the pit before the second explosion occurred. They both descended again and Hulley did very valuable service indeed, not only in the removal of the bodies, but in the hazardous work of building up the first sets of rude stoppings. He was present at the third explosion, which occurred early in the morning of the following day, and was slightly injured by bricks which were blown out of the stoppings. He also took part in the subsequent salvage operations.

It was in tending the stoppings that Mr Williamson also distinguished himself, and on several occasions he displayed rare pluck in the presence of real and imminent peril. He was not then a fully trained rescue worker, but he did a good deal of salvage work at the rescue base with the erection of the steel doors, which were used to smother out the fire.

Mr J.E.Chambers, brother of Mr W.H.Chambers, Managing Director of the collieries, not only displayed skill and courage, but splendid fortitude under affliction, for he was instrumental in saving life in the stricken mine after he knew that his only son, Mr Douglas Chambers, the clever and promising young manager of Denaby Main had perished. He recovered from a heap of bodies two men who he discovered to be breathing, and they were subsequently restored.

Walter Prince was also personally bereaved by the terrible disaster, rendered splendid service by an act of coolness which undoubtedly saved a considerable body of rescue workers. He discovered a fresh outbreak of fire, which, but for his efforts as extinguishing agent, would have cut off a number of men who were busy with the pulmoters endeavouring to restore animation in Mr Charles Bury and others, who had just survived the second explosion.

Amongst these was Sergeant Winch, of the Wath rescue station, who mainly directed the rescue operation, and who was a host in himself that day, working for his life at the pulmotors while in momentary expectation of further explosions. He also went down the pit and assisted in rescue work daily for a number of weeks after the disaster.

That in brief, is a story of how these men came to earn their medals, and they were

Sergeant Winch

J Edwin Chambers

summoned to attend his Majesty's counsel at Buckingham Palace on Tuesday morning to receive the medals at the hands of the King.

AT THE PALACE.

They travelled down on Monday night, and on Tuesday morning presented themselves at the Home Office, in Whitehall, where were foregathered a number of other cloth-capped heroes from the Midlands and the North, bound for the Palace on a similar errand..

They were escorted by a home office official through St James's Park to the Palace, where they were ushered into a large anteroom. In all there were 23 of these courageous colliery workers waiting on the King's pleasure. The Cadeby party arived the Palace at 11, and after a wait of about 40 minutes they were transferred to a smaller anteroom by way of which they were ushered into the Presence chamber. Small hooks had been attached to the lapels of their coats to facilitate the act of decoration, and after making their bow they stood at attention to receive the congratulations of the King, which were contained in a few well chosen expressions of goodwill.

As he attached each medal to the person of its recipient, His Majesty listened to a brief account of the circumstances in which the medal was earned. He did not curiously enough, make any reference to his own experience of the disaster, the unique circumstances that he was in the district at the time, and with the Queen, visited the colliery on the evening of the day of desolation.

The South Yorkshire heroes received their medals and retired from the chamber with a dutiful bow. The King, who was dressed for travelling, at the conclusion of the ceremony of decorating the industrial heroes, left the Palace for King's Cross, en route for Studley Royal, near Ripon, where he has gone to shoot.

The Edward Medal is a striking and handsome piece of coinage.

The front of the medal bears the simple inscription : " For Courage," and on the obverse side, in the case of the Cadeby party, a representation of an under – ground working is stamped.

The name of the owner is stamped, as in the case of war medals, on the rim.

Mexborough Times December 20th 1913.

Brave Men In London.
At Palace To Receive Their Awards.

Some of the party of Cadeby Main Heroes outside the gates of Buckingham Palace after receiving their Life-Saving Medals from King George V.

On Tuesday, shortly after noon, his Majesty the King presented the silver life saving medal of the Order of St. John of Jerusalem in England, to seventeen men, for gallantry displayed in the Cadeby Main mine on July 9th 1912, on the occasion of the disastrous explosion which resulted in the death of eighty-nine men.
The names singled out for this very considerable honour are as follows :-
The Rev. Sidney Featherstone Hawkes – Vicar of Denaby Main.
Dr. James Forster – Conisbrough.
Dr. Dhun Feroze – Formerly of Denaby Main, now of Leek, Staffordshire.
Basil Henry Pickering – Manager of Wath Main Colliery.
Edward Feeney – Deputy, Denaby Main.
William R. Goodwin – Deputy, Denaby Main.
Benjamin Mansbridge – Avenue Road, Wath-on-Dearne, Machine-man.
Fred Adamson – Deputy, Denaby Main
Joseph Blenkiron – Deputy, Denaby Main.
Harry Rockcliffe – Dataller, Denaby Main.
Albert Wall – Dataller, Denaby Main.
Walter Wilkinson – Deputy, Denaby Main.
George Wilding – Collier, Denaby Main.
Joseph Bucknall – Deputy, Denaby Main.
George Milnes – Under-manager, Denaby Main.
Tom Soar – Formerly of Denaby Main, now of Hendnesford, Staffordshire, Surveyor.

History
The history of this batch of honours has several interesting features. The medals were not applied for, nor in any way sought by the recipients. The Order itself was the first to move on the matter.

Sir Herbert Perrott, Secretary-General of the Grand Priory of the Order of St. John, approached the Archbishop of York, who is prelate of the Order, and who it will be remembered, was a frequent visitor to the stricken district during and immediately after the explosions, with a request that he should institute inquiries as to what life-saving had been carried out.

His Grace promptly appointed a local committee, which investigated the whole of the circumstances, watched the proceedings at the inquests and Home Office inquiry, and finally selected the seventeen names which were approved by the Order.

Why Heroes Are Overlooked.

It may be here mentioned that the selection of these worthy people for special recognition and also the recipients of the Edward Medal who figured at the Palace a few months ago in similar circumstances, has given rise to a certain amount of heart-burning among those who, probably rightly, consider that they did just as much to entitle them to decoration as have their more fortunate colleagues. But the granting of St. John's silver life-saving medal is hedged about with rather stringent conditions which would disqualify many a brave deed done in the mine during that awful time, from recognition.

For instance, to gain this medal it must be proved the person in respect of whom application was made knew there was danger at the time, and he must have saved or attempted to save, a living person. No amount of heroism in the recovery of dead bodies would count. Further the claimant must be able to produce the signature of an eye-witness, and the good faith of that eye-witness must be guaranteed by the counter-signature of his employer or the nearest clergyman or magistrate. So that although much high courage displayed in the Cadeby pit has necessarily gone unrecognised, it is because of the conditions under which this particular medal is granted. Everybody who was entitled under those conditions to a medal has been included in the list, with the exception of one unidentified hero, whose identity cannot be discovered.

A special feature of Tuesday's Royal presentation was the fact that never before in the history of the Order of St. John has this medal been bestowed by the reigning monarch. It has always been presented by the Grand Prior, or, in his absence, by some lower official of the Order, so that the Cadeby party were doubly honoured.

All the recipients, with the exception of Mr. Tom Soar and Dr. Feroze, who have since gone to reside in Staffordshire, hail from the immediate neighbourhood of the colliery, and as Mr. Tom Soar came home for the week-end prior to going down to London for his medal, Dr. Feroze alone made the journey from another district.

The Rev. S.F. Hawkes went in advance of the main party, and returned after them, because he had a good deal of private business to transact, including an interview with the Bishop of Kensington. He went down on Monday morning, and the main body of the party left by the 3-45 from Doncaster, arriving in King's Cross at seven o'clock. They spent an enjoyable evening, some of them patronising the Coliseum, while others went to see " Joseph and his Brethren " at His Majesty's theatre.

The Drive To The Palace.

They spent the night at a temperance hotel near King's Cross and at ten o'clock on Tuesday morning met by arrangement at the Grand Hotel in Northumberland Avenue, where Mr. William Henry Morgan, an Esquire of the Order, met them, having been deputed to act as their guide and host. The party were driven in a motor-bus to the gates of Buckingham Palace. By a stroke of good fortune they arrived there at the moment when the Irish Guards were changing guard, and they were able to witness what always is an interesting spectacle. They were much 'taken' with the huge Irish deerhound, which is the mascot of the regiment. Soon they were joined by Colonel Sir Herbert Perrott, who, after talking to them a little while, conducted them into the large entrance hall of the palace. There they found other people, mostly groups of individuals waiting to be decorated. Theirs was the only party of any considerable size, and they were drawn up in single file on one side of the hall.

The King Remembers.
Soon Viscount Knutsford, Sub-Prior of the Order, came and talked with them a little while, and then they were summoned to go forward into another large hall, where they waited for about half-an-hour. They were the last party to be introduced to the King, and while they were waiting each man had a fastener placed in the lapel of his coat, with a ring attached for the greater convenience of hooking on the medals. When their turn for presentation came, they marched forward in single file through an open door into a smaller room. The King was standing in the middle of the room, dressed in ordinary morning attire. The Cadeby party marched silently past His Majesty, and then drew up in a line in front of him and stood at attention.

The King spoke a few words suitable to the occasion. His voice was a little husky and indistinct, but the effect of what he said was that he thanked them for the bravery they had displayed during the disaster, and was pleased to present the medals. " I remember the occasion only too well myself," he said.

There were with the King during the presentation :-
Viscount Knutsford.
The Right Hon. R. McKenna (Home Secretary).
The Right Hon. Sidney Buxton (President of the Board of Trade).
The Lord Loch (Lord in Waiting).
Mr. Harry L. Verney (Master of the Household).
Major, the Lord Charles Fitzmaurice (Groom and Equerry in Waiting).
Mr. R.F. Reynard (Secretary and Registrar of the Edward Medal).
Colonel Sir Herbert Perrott (Secretary-General of the Order of St. John).

The Medal

The silver medal of life-saving is handsomely designed. On the obverse side there is an engraving of the Maltese cross and lions, the emblems of the Order, and the inscription : " For service in the cause of humanity."
On the converse side is the engraving of the wort plant, another emblem of the Order, with the inscription : " Awarded by the Grand Priory of the Hospital of St. John of Jerusalem in England."
The medals were all set out in order on a scarlet cushion placed on a table close to the King's hand, and His Majesty, after thus briefly addressing the party
Walked down the line, hooking every man his medal on, and shaking him by the hand, a Court official following with the cushion and the supply of medals.

Lunch At Holborn.

The ceremony over, a word of command was given, and the party marched briskly out of the Royal presence by another door.

Outside the Palace, they were besieged by press-men and photographers, and after the group photograph was taken, Mr. W.H. Morgan, who was kindness itself and was evidently anxious to give his guests the best possible time, again took charge of them, and they re-embarked upon the motor-bus, by means of which they were able to drive round a few of the sights of London. Then at half-past one, they repaired to the Holborn Restaurant, where they lunched at the expense of the Order, a special menu having been prepared, and each man brought away with his menu, as a memento of a very happy occasion.

At the conclusion of a most excellent luncheon, Mr. Morgan gave an interesting little speech on the history of the Order, and submitted two toasts, those of the King, and of H.R.H. the Duke of Connaught, the Grand Prior, both of which were enthusiastically received.

Mr. George Milnes, the under-manger of Denaby Main, moved a vote of thanks to Mr. Morgan, Mr. Wilkinson seconded, and the Rev. S.F. Hawkes and Mr. Basil Pickering also spoke, Mr. Morgan responding suitably.

After lunch the party scattered for an hour or two, and most of them caught the 5-45 train for home, arriving in Denaby Main at ten o'clock, after having had the time of their lives.

The medals, it should be mentioned, have yet to have the names of their owners inscribed on the edge.

The Vicar Down The Pit.

Rev S.F. Hawkes

With reference to the medal awarded to the Rev. S.F. Hawkes, it has been, incorrectly stated that he administered extreme unction and spiritual consolation to the dying. The rev. gentleman went down the mine to do so, having warned the pit was liable to 'go off' again, but he found all the survivors in a condition of unconsciousness, and he contented himself with rendering practical aid, helping Dr. Forster with his medical appliances, and doing anything his hand found to do.

Dr. Feroze also worked hard on the survivors in another part of the mine. This took place between the second and third explosion.

The medals won by the Vicar the Rev. S.F. Hawkes, Dr. Forster, Dr. Feroze, C. Wilding, A. Sykes, W. Wilkinson, B. Pickering, T.A. Soar, A. Wall, H. Rockcliffe, J. Bucknall, and G. Milnes, were for work done on the day of the disaster and the two succeeding days.

The medals given to W.R. Goodwin, E. Feeney, F. Adamson, J. Blenkiron, and B. Mansbridge, were for courage displayed in saving life and attempting to save life while rescue and salvage operations were being conducted by the parties working with the apparatus, the instances arising at intervals after the disaster.

The party had an excellent outing, and returned well pleased with the nature of their reception, and the arrangements which had been thoughtfully made for their comfort.

The Cadeby Medal

The 'Cadeby Medal' is unique in the annals of mining, in that it was awarded to women for their work in the explosion at Cadeby Main Colliery in 1912.

Each of the lady recipients of the 'Cadeby Medal' were members of the Denaby Main Nursing Division of the St Johns Ambulance Brigade and they were:

Mrs H Yates; Mrs H Kirkby; Mrs F M Grainger; Elsie May Ashworth (later Mrs Cooke, Nursing Sperintendant at Denaby Main); Mrs E Laycock; Mrs Hilton; Mrs Cavanagh

Some of whom went underground from Tuesday morning working through until Wednesday night, helping with First Aid and comforting the injured.
They returned to the Pit on Friday morning to give more help. Other remained on the surface to clean the dirt from the bodies of the dead men as they were recovered and brought to the surface to the temporary mortuary there.

Mrs Harriet Kirkby was born in 1849. She was a member of the Denaby Main Nursing Division of the St Johns Ambulance Brigade which she joined in 1909. She received the Cadeby Medal for service during the aftermath of the disaster. She was also the first woman in the South East Area of the West Hiding of Yorkshire to be made a Serving Sister of the Grand Priory in the British Realm of the Most Venerable Order of St John of Jerusalem in 1924. She lived at 63 Bolton Street and was an active member of the Denaby Main Nursing Division until her death in June 1937, aged 88.

Elsie May Cooke was born 23rd May 1896 in Denaby Main. As a young lady of 16 Elsie May Ashworth as she was then called, was awarded the Gold engraved medal, the Cadeby Medal for assisting at the explosion.
Mrs Cooke began her studies with the nursing division of the St John's Ambulance Brigade in 1912. She progressed to Ambulance Officer in 1925, Lady Divisional Superintendant in 1939 and in 1938 became Secretary of the Division and also later treasurer. For many years she was Captain of the Denaby Main Nursing Competition team.

Mrs H. Yates joined the Denaby Main Division in 1909 and received the 'Cadeby Medal' for her work during the aftermath of the explosion. Mrs Yates was responsible for the formation of the Nursing Division in 1916 and became the Lady Superintendant of the Mexborough Nursing Division.

CADEBY COLLIERY DISASTER RELIEF FUND

The disaster left 63 widows and 132 children fatherless.
A relief fund was quickly established and over 300 contributors raised a total of £9,000.

From the fund an amount of 5 shillings (25p) weekly was paid to each widow and 1 shilling weekly for each child until they reached 14 years.

The trustees of the fund were by notables such as the Earl of Yarborough and Viscount Halifax amongst others and the fund was administered by the local clergy, colliery management and local professsionals

Church	£	s	d
Archbishop of York	50	0	0
Denaby Church	21	2	10
Rawmarsh Parish Church	13	9	6
Melton Parish Church	13	7	9
Church Parade Royston	12	3	4
York Minster Offertory	11	0	0
Rev G.N.Ward	10	0	0
St Marys, Doncaster	8	1	5
Tankersley Parish Church	7	13	6
Mexborough Cong Church	7	4	0
Conisbro' Parish Church	7	2	7
St Helen's , Thurnscoe	5	16	3
Canon Bateman	5	0	0
Rev J M Bury	5	0	0
St Johns Church, Balby	4	11	2
Collection (Rev. W.Sykes)	4	3	9
Wath Parish Church	3	16	3
Concert, Weslyan, Pilsley	2	13	0
Sprotbro' Cadeby Church	2	13	0
Elsecar Church Collection	2	10	0
Sheffield Church Football	2	2	0
Thurnscoe Bible Class	2	2	0
Eastwood Weslyen Miss	1	15	1
Cardiston , Shrewsbury	1	9	0
Bawtry Parish Church	1	7	4
Rev W.A.Strawbridge	1	1	0
Rev A Shakesby, Filey	1	1	0
Rev S H Spooner, Mexb	1	1	0
Rev W E Wigfall, Beverly	1	1	0
Attercliffe Brotherhood	1	0	0
St Hildas Thurnscoe		18	8
South Elmsall Church		18	3
WakefieldMount Zion		10	0
Church School, Pelton		10	9

Companies	£	s	d
Logan & Hemingway	41	9	0
Messrs Kilner Bros	25	0	0
North British Wagon Co	25	0	0
Pyman Ball & Co Ltd	21	0	0
Per Leng & Co	20	17	4
Grocock's Wagon Co Ltd	10	10	0
J Whitaker & Co Ltd	10	10	0
Nobel's Explosive Co	10	10	0
Wm. Mathwin and Son	10	10	0
Osmond & Son	10	0	0
British Westfalite Ltd	5	5	0
Mexboro & Swinton Tram Co	5	5	0
Renton Holdsworth and Co	5	5	0
W.Thompson, Huddersfield	5	5	0
India Rubber Co Ltd	5	0	0
Isaac Bently & Co ltd	5	0	0
Robinson Bros, Conisbrough	5	0	0
H.L.Brown & Sons	3	3	0
Bells United Asbestos	2	2	0
Bruce & Sturrock, Dundee	2	2	0
E & E.H. Jubb	2	2	0
H C Chambers, Sheffield	2	2	0
J.L.Seaton & Co Hull	2	2	0
Messrs R.D.Nichol & Co	2	2	0
Jno Clark & Co., Sheffield	1	1	0
Beans' Express Limited		8	0
E.M.L.		2	6

Breweries & Pubs	£	s	d
Whitworth, Son & Nephew	200	0	0
Ind Coope & Co Ltd	25	0	0
Mappins Masbro Brewery	20	0	0
Wm. Younger & Co Ltd	10	0	0
Chas Day, Plough Inn	5	5	0
Conisbrough Castle W.M.C.	5	5	0
Mexborough & Dist Lic Vict	5	5	0
Sheffield Free Brewery	5	5	0
Wharncliffe Silkstone Club	5	5	0
South Kirkby Coll Ath Club	5	0	0
Clarence Hotel Rotherham	1	15	0
Bolton WMC	1	0	0
Queens Hotel Pontefract		14	6

Organisations

Organisations	£	s	d
Cooperative Wholesale Soc	250	0	0
Denaby Co operative Soc	100	0	0
Kilnhurst Coop	10	0	0
Manchester Druids	10	0	0
Denaby Boy Scouts	8	12	6
Sheffield Drapers Asn	6	13	6
Sheffield Druids	5	0	0
Folkstone St Johns Amb	4	16	0
Montagu Lodge Druids	3	0	0
Swinton Boys Scouts	2	10	0
Manchester Oddfellows	2	2	0
Battieford Boy Scouts,Mirield	1	18	9
Swinton Temperance Band	1	13	7
Maltby Ramblers	1	13	0
Birmingham Small Arms Club	1	5	7
Pontefract I L p	1	2	0
Derby Society of Engineers	1	1	0
Mexborough Shop assistants		10	6
A.S.R.S. (South Elmsall)		10	0
Doncaster Socialist Party		7	9

Overseas

	£	s	d
Hawes Bay Tribune, N.Z.	25	13	0
Waimate Times, N.Z.	23	1	4
Denaby Men in Canada	5	10	0
Kingston Coll Vancouver	1	5	0

Collieries

	£	s	d
Hulton Coll Explsn Fund	1,050	0	0
Micklefield Coll Explosion	1,000	0	0
SY Coal Trade Assoc	1,000	0	0
Cortonwood Colliery Co	51	14	3
Clerical Denaby & Cadeby	23	7	6
Yorkshire Coll Enginemen	10	0	0

Schools

	£	s	d
Kiveton Park Council	2	0	0
South Elmsall School	1	9	0
Elsecar National School	1	3	6
Moorthorpe Junior School		4	3

Theatres

	£	s	d
Empire, Goldthorpe	16	13	6
Royal Electric Theatre	10	10	6
Wombwell Hippodrome	10	0	8
Highfield &W Comic Band	7	7	0
Chesterfield Corporation	5	5	0
Garden Street Picture Hall	2	2	0
Mexborough Theatre	2	2	0
"The Dandies", Morcmbe	1	7	6
Imperial Hall, Dulwich	1	4	4

Individuals

Individuals	£	s	d
J Buckingham Pope	1,000	0	0
Captain Pope	500	0	0
F.J.O.Montague Esq	500	0	0
Mayor of Doncaster	176	18	7
S Arthur Peto	105	0	0
Charles Thellusson, Esq	100	0	0
Earl and Countess Yarboro	100	0	0
H.M. the King	100	0	0
J C Cunningham	100	0	0
Mrs. Godfrey Walker, Exeter	100	0	0
W.H.Chambers, Denaby	100	0	0
Sir John Horsfall, Bart	59	0	0
H.M. the Queen	50	0	0
Lady Church	50	0	0
Sir Arthur Church	50	0	0
W W Warde-Aldam Esq	50	0	0
Earl of Harewood	25	0	0
Mrs J Across, Rugby	25	0	0
J.W.Hattersley, Mexboro	20	0	0
Lord Mexboro	20	0	0
Kilner Bros Workmen	15	7	1
Mrs Coldwell Sandwich	12	10	0
Mrs Kearsley, Sandwich	12	10	0
Mrs M K Coldwell	12	10	0
Ms E M Kearsley	12	10	0
Alexander Nisbet, Lincs	10	10	0
D.M.Nicholson	10	10	0
J. Fieldsend	10	10	0
Lord Mayor of Sheffield	10	10	0
Master Cutler of Sheffield	10	10	0
A R Harding	10	0	0
George Wilkie, Doncaster	10	0	0
H.C.Else	10	0	0
N B Laidlaw	10	0	0
T R Nicholas	10	0	0
Dr. McCall	5	5	0
F.Ogley Esq.	5	5	0
Sam Spencer Esq.	5	5	0
V Harrdt, Paris	5	5	0
W Williams	5	5	0
W.J.Gibbs Esq	5	5	0
Wm Brennand	5	5	0
Bishop of Sheffield	5	0	0
E A & F Clayton	5	0	0
J.H.T.Child	5	0	0
Lasy Worlsey	5	0	0
Lord Worlsey	5	0	0
Miss M Pontifex 'Daily Mail	5	0	0
Mr G White, High Melton	5	0	0
Mr S F Skipworth	5	0	0
Mr. Frank Allen, Doncaster	5	0	0
Mrs. Wilkie, Doncaster	5	0	0
Viscount Chetwynd	5	0	0
W.W.Nicholas (Hull)	5	0	0

Individuals (contd)	£	s	d
C.E.Vickers Esq	3	3	0
Mr & Mrs John Hoyle	3	3	0
W E Carrington	3	3	0
Mrs Beardshall (Wombwell)	2	16	0
Miss Anne E Hodgkinson	2	10	0
Miss Mary Hodgkinson	2	10	0
Edlington New Village	2	10	0
A Walter	2	2	0
Dr C.G.Porter, Sheffield	2	2	0
G.J.Hawkes, Pilton	2	2	0
Mrs Banks	2	2	0
Mrs. C.H.Johnson	2	2	0
Dr Burman, Wath	2	0	0
Mrs Yarker, Hunamby	2	0	0
Inspctor Fairburn's Testimnial	2	0	0
Harry Beaumont, Wath	1	15	0
A S Wadsworth, Denaby Main	1	10	0
Jury at the Inquest	1	5	0
A Sympathiser, Wath	1	1	0
Capt A.Weigall M.P.	1	1	0
D.V.E.Dodsworth	1	1	0
Dr. W.G.McArthur, Thirsk	1	1	0
E J Chennell	1	1	0
E L Appleyard	1	1	0
E Roberts	1	1	0
Ernest Wilson, Doncaster	1	1	0
F Gill	1	1	0
F Hadwen	1	1	0
Harry Humphrey	1	1	0
In memory of Ellen Paske	1	1	0
J Wood	1	1	0
Miss Gertrude Drabble	1	1	0
Mrs Hoyle Senior	1	1	0
Mrs J.H.Wood	1	1	0
Mrs Sutherland	1	1	0
Mrs. M.C.Liddell	1	1	0
R.A.Wall	1	1	0
W H Blore	1	1	0
E Tunnicliffe	1	0	0
G.W.W.Way	1	0	0
In Memory of Lilian	1	0	0
J.H.Roberts	1	0	0
Miss Bateson	1	0	0
Mr. J.E.M.Greaves	1	0	0
Scotlan!'	1	0	0
The Children of Bawtry		15	9
Anon		11	6
F.Mannes		10	6
Anon Sheffield		10	0
Anon Workman, Birmingham		10	0
J.H.Brocklesby		10	0
Manx		10	0
Mis Blaseby		10	0
R Wright		10	0
Wm Wright		10	0

£		s	d
Andrew Stephenson		10	6
Jas. Stansfield		10	6
Miss Kent, Birmingham		10	6
Mr.W.A.Twelves		10	6
Miss A.Tunnicliffe		10	0
Mrs J.H.E.Brock		10	0
Mrs.H.Miller		10	0
The Great Athelda		10	0
A few friends, London		9	6
Mrs Moore & Miss Moore		9	0
Billy Buchanan		7	0
Mrs Barnard		7	0
A miner		5	0
E.Shuker		5	0
J.Royston		5	0
Miss M Witty		5	0
Anon (Harewood)		5	0
F.I.Bray		5	0
Misses Prift		5	0
Mr. R.J.Kilgour, Burslem		5	0
Mrs F.E.Edwards		5	0
Mrs Wood, Oundle		5	0
W.Dryden		5	0
Miss Adcock, Chichester		4	0
Mrs Reynolds		3	0
'Sympathy', Ilkley		3	0
A Subscriber, Western Morning		2	6
Miss Lily Finney, a servant girl		2	6
G.W.Middleton (Postman)		2	6
Miss Fretwell		2	0
Miss Stevenson, Wath		1	0
Miss Thompson, Halifax		1	0
T Harris, 'a working man's mite		1	0

Note:
In pre Decimal days the £ was subdivided into shillings (s) and pence (d).
there was 20 shillings to a £ and 12 pence to each shilling

The People who Died

Forename	Surname	Age	Occupation	Address
William	Ackroyd	49	Dataller	Alexandra Terrace, Conisbrough
Charles	Alderson	25	Dataller	2. Sheardown Street, Hexthorpe
James	Beach	44	Dataller	42 Barnborough Street, Denaby
Willie	Berry	47	Deputy	Tickhill Street, Denaby Main
Joseph	Boycott	67	Dataller	30 Ivanhoe Road, Conisbrough
Robert Peel	Bungard	21	Filler	10 Willow Street, Conisbrough
James	Burdekin	24	Dataller	8 Firbeck Street, Denaby Main
Thomas	Burns	48	Dataller	21 Marr Street, Denaby Main
Charles	Bury	35	Manager	Red House, Denaby Main
John William	Carlton	38	Deputy	21 Tickhill Square, Denaby Main
Arthur	Carroll	25	Dataller	38 Loversall Street, Denaby Main
Douglas	Chambers	28	Manager	" Peveril " Conisbro'.
Robert William	Chapman	37	Dataller	7 Dufton's Row, Conisbrough.
Thomas	Cody	32	Collier	76 Clifton Street, Denaby Main
Eli	Croxall	49	Under Manager	28 Tickhill Square, Denaby Main
Herbert	Cusworth	39	Under Manager	Cadeby Villas
Wiliam Charles	Davis	26	Filler & Driver	7 Drabbles Yard, Conisbrough.
George	Denton	21	Dataller	42 Firbeck Street, Denaby Main
Willie	Dove	42	Dataller	35 Gardens Lane, Conisbrough.
Arthur	Dungworth	24	Dataller	13 March Gate, Conisbrough
Robert Neil	Eddington	24	Dataller	Chapel Lane, Conisbrough.
Sydney	Ellis	32	Surveyor	Holywell Lane, Conisbrough.
Phillip George	Evans	48	Dataller	68 Annerley Street, Denaby Main.
Thomas Emrys	Evans	22	Mining Student	Wales.
Thomas	Fleck	24	Dataller	8 Holywell Street, Conisbrough
John	Fletcher	66	Dataller	40 Edlington Street, Denaby Main
Charles William	Fletcher	29	Dataller	47 Maltby Street, Denaby Main
Arthur	Flynn	21	Driver	109 Tickhill Street, Denaby Main
Joseph Benjmn	Fox	24	Driver	66 Earnshaw Lane, Conisbrough
William	Frankland	43	Dataller	5 Rowena Row, Conisbrough
Richard	Gascoyne	22	Driver	78 Loversall Street, Denaby Main
William H	Godsmark	28	Dataller	65 Lime Grove, Conisbrough
William	Green	26	Filler	9 Marr Street, Denaby Main
Tobias	Hancock	29	Onsetter	Yew Terrace, Low Road,Conisbro'
Michael	Hayden	30	Dataller	77 Firbeck Street, Denaby Main
Edward	Henderson	41	Collier	65 Balby Street, Denaby Main
Edward	Henderson	41	Collier	65 Balby Street, Denaby Main
George	Heptinstall	28	Corporal	85 Clifton Street, Denaby Main.
Henry Richard	Hewitt	45	Hm Insp of Mines	Sheffield.
George	Hindson (Hinton)	25	Dataller	Cadeby Village
Frederick William	Horsfall	21	Surveyor	149 Tickhill Street , Denaby Main.
William	Humphries	33	Deputy	Tickhill Square, Denaby Main
Charles Albert	Hunt	28	Dataller	97 Clifton Street, Denaby Main
Samuel	Jackson	30	Assistant Deputy	102, Doncaster Road, Denaby Main
Charles	Johnson	33	Deputy	78 Cliff View, Denaby Main
Matthew	Jordan	52	Dataller	61 Loversall Street, Denaby Main

Forename	Surname	Age	Occupation	Address
John William	Kelsall	26	Deputy	66 Ravenfield Street, Denaby Main
William	Lambert	29	Dataller	75 Loversall Street, Denaby Main
John	Marrow (Marsden)	30	Dataller	62 Loversall Street, Denaby Main
James	McDonagh	49	Collier	17 Cliff View, Denaby Main
John	Mulhearn	27	Collier	22 Adwick Street, Denaby Main
Martin	Mulrooney	35	Dataller	Kirby Street, Mexborough
Herbert	Neal	38	Onsetter	2 School Terrace, Conisbrough
Percy Edgar	Nicholson	18	Driver	5 Beech Hill, Conisbrough
Jarratt	Phillips	44	Deputy	12 Wood View, Denaby Main
William Henry	Pickering	53	Hm Inspctr Mines	Lawn House , Doncaster
Charles Edward	Prince	23	Deputy	The Glen, Mexborough
Charles William P	Radley	22	Filler	75 Balby Street, Denaby Main
Frederick	Richardson	50	Deputy	81 Tickhill Square, Denaby Main
Cyrus	Rodgers	28	Collier	48 Ivanhoe Road, Conisbrough
Joseph	Roodhouse	38	Dataller	127 Park Road, Conisbrough
Joseph	Ross	37	Collier	64 Northcliffe, Conisbrough
Arthur Edward	Rowell	34	Dataller	Wadsworth Street, Denaby Main
Samuel Thomas	Sanders	51	Dataller	60 Cliff View Road, Denaby Main
Joseph	Shuttleworth	47	Corporal	5 Cross Street, Conisbrough
John	Smith	58	Collier	65 Firbeck Street, Denaby Main
James	Springthorpe	19	Surrveyor	143 Tickhill Street, Denaby Main
George	Steadman (Young)	31	Dataller	86 Blythe Street, Denaby Main
Frederick	Stone	34	Dataller	39 Warmsworth Street, Denaby
Thomas	Stribley	35	Dataller	44 Edlington Street, Denaby Main
Willie	Summerscales	37	Deputy	25 Tickhill Street, Denaby Main
Timothy Smith	Talbot	28	Filler	125 Tickhill Street, Denaby Main
John William	Tarbrook	23	Contracter	30 Firbeck Street, Denaby Main
Henry	Thompson	21	Filler	2 Sprotborough St., Denaby Main
James	Thompson	54	Dataller	6 Adams Yard, Mexborough
Gilbert Young	Tickle	34	H.M. Inspector	Doncaster.
Charles Edgar	Tuffrey	20	Driver	30 Northcliffe Road, Conisbrough
Edmund Jesse	Tuffrey	22	Corporal	30 Northcliffe Road, Conisbrough
Joseph	Turner	26	Dataller	66 Warmsworth Strt, Denaby Main
William Henry	Wallace	56	Dataller	14 Barnborough Street, DenabyMn
Thomas	Walsh	41	Dataller	7 Wood View, Denaby Main
Frank	Walton	39	Deputy	10 Strafforth Terrace, Denaby Main
Benjamin	Ward	30	Collier	1 Tickhill Street, Denaby Main
William David	Waters	31	Driver	28 Firbeck Street, Denaby Main
Samuel	Webster	41	Deputy	19 Ivanhoe Road, Conisbrough
George	Whitton	32	Deputy	24 Maltby Street, Denaby Main
Thomas Samuel	Williams	36	Deputy	55 Maltby Street, Denaby Main
Richard	Wimpenny	56	Deputy	16 Tickhill Square, Denaby Main
Thomas	Wraithmell	53	Onsetter	17 Tickhill Square, Denaby Main

Died after the disaster

Forename	Surname	Address
Frank	Wood	Braithwell Street, Denaby Main
James	Burns	Wath
James	Springthorpe	143 Tickhill Street, Denaby Main

The Victims and Heroes

Information from the 1911 Census is in italics or tabular form.
Unless otherwise shown all other information is from the 'Mexborough and Swinton Times'

William Ackroyd

Alexander Terrace, Conisbrough

William was born on September 6th, 1862 at Edlington near Doncaster, the 5th child of James and Mary Ackroyd He married Mary Walker of Darrington on March 26th 1889 at St Peter's Church, Edlington. William and Mary had seven children during their marriage. They were Oswald Walter; Annie; William; Thomas Henry; Frederick; Mary and James.

William met an early death at the age of 49 in the Cadeby Pit Disaster. At the time, we are told, that William was off work suffering from a broken toe. When he heard of an explosion at the Cadeby Colliery where he worked, William went to assist in the rescue operation. During the rescue a second explosion occurred in which William lost his life. The explosion was so severe that William could only be identified by his belt and broken toe.

William was buried on July 14th 1912 at Conisbrough Cemetery. Other members of his family are buried with him.

Many thanks to Carol Ackroyd for the above photograph and information.

Charles Alderson

2. Sheardown Street, Hexthorpe.

Charles Alderson was a 25 year old Dataller, killed in the first explosion

James Beach

42 Barnborough Street, Denaby Main

One of the hardest cases is that of the widow of James Beach, who was killed in the first explosion, and whose body was one of the earliest to be discovered. He leaves a widow and 12 children, the youngest of whom is two months old. The oldest is Dan Beech, a married man, who keeps goal for Crystal Palace, and formerly was goalkeeper for Mexborough Town.

Letter to South Yorkshire Times from Irene Newton (granddaughter) in 2003
Sir, I do hope you will be remembering the men from Denaby and Conisbrough who died in the Cadeby Colliery disaster in 1912. My grandfather was 42 years of age and left a wife and 12 children - the youngest Albert Beach was two months old.The widows received 5/- (25p) per week and the children 1/- (5p) per week until the age of 14. My granny had that 5/- until she died in 1938. As the money in the fund reduced, the remaining widows were told in 1934 that they would have to go on Parish Relief and receive 4/- per week. My granny didn't like the idea of going on what we call today Social Security and protested. Eventually, after much discussion, the 16 widows were given the 5/- (25p) per week which cost the fund

£4 per week given by the men who delivered the coal in the area.
What would people think of that today ? We who were living in those days know the meaning
of independence and hard work. I am 91 now and still remember those 1920/30/40 years.

Irene Newton

Willie Berry
84 Tickhill Street, Denaby Main

Funeral of Mr. Wm. Berry

The remains of the late Mr. Willie Berry were interred last Tuesday afternoon, 24th September, at the Conisbrough Cemetery. Deep signs of respect were witnessed as the cortege wended its way down Tickhill Street, the blinds being drawn. Prior to the interment at Conisbrough, a service was held at the Denaby Parish Church and was largely attended by friends. This was conducted by the Rev S.F.Hawkes, assisted by the Rev. J.W. Tunnicliffe. The Rev. S.F.Hawkes officiated at the graveside.

Mr. Berry was a well-known and highly respected man and was buried with every manifestation of deep regret.

The St John's Ambulance Brigade (of which deceased was a member) were in attendance, under the supervision of Sergeant Major Power and 4th Officer W.V.Simpson. The members of the Nursing Division were also in attendance. The coffin, which was borne by members of the Brigade, was of polished pitch pine, panelled and with brass furniture.

The chief mourners include: Mrs. Berry (widow), Mr. A.E.Berry, Mr and Mrs. John Berry, Miss Popsy Berry (grand-daughter), Miss Berry and Master Jesse Berry, Mr George Mapes (Chesterfield), Mrs Crookes, Mrs B.Berry, Mr A.Berry (nephew), Mr B.Berry, Miss E.Berry (neice), Miss Emma Berry, Mr. and Mrs. J.Scott, Mr and Mrs A.Rothery, Mr W.Rothery and Miss Rothery, Mr and Mrs. A Hilton, Mr. & Mrs Allen Hilton, Mr & Mrs W.Hilton, Mr & Mrs W.Hilton, Mr & Mrs A.Smalley (Wombwell Main), Mr & Mrs B.Hilton, Mrs Donovan (Dewsbury) Mr & Mrs T.Mitchell (Bolton on Dearne), Mrs Hayes (Dodworth), Mrs Beevors (Darton), Mrs Lumb, Mrs Fallas (Horbury), Mr & Mrs Potts (Wombwell) Mr W.Smalley (Wath), Mr F.Diggle (Wombwell), Mr & Mrs Wallace (Maltby), Miss Milburn (Newcastle), Mr & Mrs Stanger (Stairfoot), Mr & MRs W.Johnson, Mrs J.Cooper, Mrs F.Barlowe, Mrs E.Wells (Conisbrough), Mrs Richardson, Mr J.Milage, Mr James Roberts, Mr G.Haigh and Mr T.W.Mosby, also members of the Conisbrough branch of the Sheffield Order of Druids.

Wreaths were sent from "Wife", "Family", "Topsy", "Cadeby Rescue Team" Mr & Mrs E.Dutton, Mr & Mrs R.Munting, Mrs B.Berry, Mrs Barlowe, Mrs Hemsworth, Mr & Mrs Smalley, Mr & Mrs Corney and flowers from Mr & Mrs Johnson, Mrs Alpine, Mrs Kerr, Mrs Fallas, Mrs Lumb, Mrs Crookes and Mrs Sleaford.
The whole of the funeral arrangements were efficiently carried out by Mr.G.L. Robinson

Willie Berry was 47 year old American originally from Pennsylvania and he worked as a Deputy at the Colliery. He lived with his 45 year old wife Anna, from Barugh Green. They

In loving memory of Willie Berry
who was killed in the Cadeby disaster July 9th 1912
Interred Sept 24th 1912 Aged 47 years
Also John George Berry Father of the above
who died April 14th 1909 aged 67 years

Joseph Boycott
30 Ivanoe Road, Conibrough

Joseph Boycott lived with his wife of 42 years Mary Boycott, aged 66. Both of them originated from Little Wenlock in Shropshire.
From the Censuses Joseph at the age of 16 in 1861 was a Stone Miner. By 1871 he had moved to Caveswell in Staffs. 1881 saw him as a Coal Miner at Pleasley in Staffs; In 1891 he was a Coal Miner and Grocer at Rawmarsh.
They were blessed with 3 children: Annie born in 1872, William born in 1879 and Mary Ann born in 1883

Robert Peel Iverna Bungard
10 Willow Street, Conisbrough

Wreaths from his wife, father and mother, his two sisters, sister and brother, aunt and uncle, Mrs. Crookes, Mr. and Mrs. W. Crookes, Mr. and Mrs. G. Neale, Mr. and Mrs. Whaley, Mr. and Mrs. C. Jackson, Mr. and Mrs. F. Crookes, Mrs. Mellor, and Mr. and Mrs Chadwick. A large number of the deceased's work mates followed.

The unfortunate young fellow was a member of the rescue party, who were killed in the second explosion. He died a hero's death.

At the time of the 1911 Census, Robert was single and lived with his parents, 41 year old Coal Miner Henry and 38 year old Lorenzo Bungard. The family originated from Shoreham in Sussex where Robert, his brother 12 year old Heny and sisters, 17 year old Annie, 15 year old Edith all were born. 8 year old Ethel was born in Doncaster.

James Burdekin
8 Firbeck Street, Denaby Main

Mourners :- Mrs. Burdekin (widow), Mr. G. Burdekin (brother), Mrs. Burdekin (mother), Mr. Albert Burdekin (brother), Mr. and Mrs. Simpson (sister and brother-in-law), Mr. and Mrs. Benton, Mr. and Mrs. Roberts, Mr. and Mrs. Oldfield Mr. and Mrs. Cheetham (brothers and sisters-in-law), Mr. C. Holmes (father), Laurie Calvert and James Henry Benton (nephews), Beatrice Benton (niece), Reginald Roberts and John W. Roberts (nephews).
Bearers – Messrs. T. Stanley, C. Smith, H. Roberts, T. Roberts, H. Barker, and E. Hammersley. Wreaths from :- " Mr. and Mrs. Roberts," " Mr. and Mrs. J.K. Sampson," " Mr. and Mrs. P. Benton," " Mr. and Mrs. Cheetham." Globe from " Wife and Child."

James Burns
Funeral of a Cadeby Hero at Wath

The funeral took place yesterday of James Burns, a member of the Manvers Main rescue party, who lost his life on Sunday last whilst assisting in the work of rescuing entombed miners from Cadeby Pit.

The deceased was well known in the Wath district, formerly a sergeant in the fourth territorial, but resigned two years ago. He was the eldest son of the late Trooper Burns of Wath. Chief mourners were: one Mr and Mrs Allen Kelly (sister and brother-in-law Wath) Mr and Mrs William Burns (brother and sister-in-law, Swinton), Mr and Mrs Charles Burns (brother and sister-in-law, Swinton), Mr Edward Burns (brother, Wath) Mr and Mrs Harold Hall sister (sister and brother-in-law) sister Isaac Smith (brother in law, Bradford), Mr George Davies (brother-in-law Mexborough), Mr and Mrs Edwards Plant (sister, Swinton) Miss Rosetta Kelly, Miss Harriet Burns, Master William Burns (nephews and nieces).

Amongst the large number of friends present were Mr A Shaw, manager of Manvers Main No 1 pit; Mr E Hampshire, and others. Members of the ambulance Brigade attended the funeral, and a contingent of the Wath territorials. The deceased was 45 years of age. The coffin was made at the Cadeby colliery and Mr WH Chambers sent a letter of condolence with the relatives, and also promised to forward an everlasting wreath. Wreaths were contributed by the relatives of the deceased; a beautiful wreath was sent by the Manvers Main rescue party; one from the Mitchell's Main party (who discovered the deceased; and also from the Hickleton Main and Wath Main rescue party. Mr Asher had charge of all the funeral arrangements. The relatives of the deceased wish to take this opportunity of thanking all friends for the sympathy extended to them in their bereavement

Story Of The Accident.

Mansbridge and Hill worked at Manvers Main No. 3, Smith and Davidson at Manvers Main No. 2, and Burns at Manvers No. 1., and the team as a whole was thoroughly trained and qualified.

The accident happened simply enough. Manvers Main and Mitchell Main were working the afternoon shift on Sunday. Denaby and Cadeby had been down in the morning, and had located the first batch of bodies, and Manvers and Mitchell had located more, bringing the total up to twelve, so that there were remaining only three unaccounted for at the time of the accident. Two teams working turn by turn, had brought two bodies out as far as the stoppings, and Manvers Main were bringing a third when Burns who was at the head of the stretcher, slipped and squeezed the air out of his breathing-bag, and Davidson, who was close by, heard him exclaim through clenched teeth : " Look sharp ! Shout to the others !"

He knew what that meant, and signalled the three at the back to go to Burns' assistance. They did so, and Davidson at the same time set off a considerable distance in search of a signal wire. While he was away Smith, Mansbridge and Hill supported Burns, and put his mouthpiece, which had been forced out of his mouth, back again, but it was forced out once more, and this time they could not restore it, for Burns was being rapidly overcome by the gas and his teeth were clenched.

So they hurried him out as quickly as they could in the direction of the stoppings, where the fresh air was, but all the time he was weakening and becoming more difficult to manage. As they were climbing over a fall of roof, he struck his head against the roof and collapsed, being unable to go any further. The other three stayed with him for a minute or two and saw that the case was hopeless. At the same time they were beset by another anxiety. Their own stock of air was nearly exhausted, and their strength was diminishing. So they decided to make a dash for safety, when a further difficulty cropped up. Hill showed signs of collapse, and Smith and Mansbridge took him between them.

When about fifty yards from the stoppings Hill collapsed, and Smith, going on, almost done, managed to struggle through the doors into the fresh air while Mansbridge, who had retained complete control of his apparatus, remained with his mate, and forced the tubes into his mouth and kept them there, feeding him on pure oxygen until the Mitchell Main party came rushing up in response to Davidson's signal.

Davidson had acted quickly and coolly and but for that signal of his, four of the five would have been wiped out by the deadly gas. He, like Mansbridge, managed to retain control of his apparatus, but all were badly exhausted when the Mitchell Main party came up, and they were assisted over the remaining fifty yards of ground, and after that the Mitchell Main men went back for Burns, whom they recovered and brought outside the stoppings. Smith and Hill were brought round fairly quickly, and eventually the four of them were able to leave the pit unassisted, and were despatched to their homes in a wagonette about twelve o'clock.

In the meantime, the Wath, Manvers Main, and Hickleton Main teams were waiting to go down on the night shift, and they, along with the Mitchell Main men and the officials, Mr. H.S. Witty (manager), Mr. S.J. Bridges (underground manager), Mr. H. Williamson (assistant manager), and Mr. George Farmer (assistant manager at Denaby Main), did all that was humanly possible for Burns by means of artificial respiration and the use of the pulmoters, but his case was hopeless, and when the doctor arrived he found him dead.

Anxious Crowds.
Mr. Chambers was quickly on the scene, and by his orders all rescue work was stopped for the night, and the teams which had been waiting to go down, returned home, along with the Mitchell Main team, which had just completed it's shift so gloriously. News of the affair soon leaked out, and it was not unnatural, in view of the tragic happenings on July 9th, that it should be wildly exaggerated. It was generally reported that there had been yet another explosion, and the death toll was variously estimated from 15 to 50.

As a consequence there was a rush of men to the pit yard and they would not be dispersed until Mr. Chambers, with the Vicar of Denaby, the Rev. F.S. Hawkes and the manager, Mr. Witty, addressed them and told them exactly what had happened, when they went away satisfied. Poor Burns was transferred at once to the mortuary in the colliery yard.

Thomas Burns
21 Marr Street, Denaby Main

Thomas Burns was a 48 year old Dataller, killed in the First explosion.
He was buried in Hoyland Cemetery on July 12th, 1912

Mr. Charles Bury
Red House, Denaby

The Last Victim. The Passing Of A Good Man.

The latest victim of the Cadeby pit disaster is probably the most bitterly lamented, and when the news spread that Mr. Charles Bury, manager of the Cadeby mine, had succumbed under his terrible ordeal at the Fullerton Hospital early on Monday morning, wounds burst open afresh and the weeping and wailing broke out anew.

For he was a greatly admired and sincerely loved man. He was the idol of the colliers, and dearly esteemed of his colleagues and his numberless personal friends. He earned great respect for his distinguished abilities as a mining engineer, and his reputation as one of the cleverest mine managers in the north of England is not seriously disputed by anyone. But more than all his loss will be felt because of the sweetness of his disposition. He had a sunny temperament gilding real strength of character and force of determination, which bound him to the hearts of the people. He was one of the most genial and jolly of men.

Received a Catholic.

In the pit and in the field of sport he was to be found keen and eager, but serene and smiling. Not a whisper of disparagement is raised throughout his wide acquaintance against his memory which will be kept fresh and green for many a year. He was young, slightly built, but hard as nails, and we all hoped against hope that he would weather through the terrible effects of the explosion. But the deadly fumes of the mine laid too heavy a toll even upon his splendid constitution, and after fighting most gamely for nearly six days it was brain-trouble that came along and put an end to a career that was developing into brilliance. Since the explosion Mr. Bury had fitful glimmerings of consciousness, and he died in a state of unconsciousness. It was a matter for general surprise that Mr. Bury had died a Roman Catholic. During his lifetime he was not prominently identified with any sect, though it was known that he had attended Mass at the Catholic Church with his aunt, Mrs. Agnes Bury, of the Red House with whom he lived, and it now appears that it was his secret desire to be received into the Body of the church, and that some time ago he expressed a wish that if anything

happened to him, Father Kavanagh should be sent for. This was done on Sunday night, and in his dying moments, the ill-fated manager of an ill-fated colliery was received a Roman Catholic, with the prospect of a Roman Catholic burial.

The Cricket Captain.

Mr. Charles Bury came to Denaby about twenty-four years ago as a mining student articled to Mr. W.H. Chambers, and he showed such excellent promise that at the early age of twenty-three he was given charge of the important colliery of Denaby Main, which he managed with rare judgement for eleven years, until in fact, last September, when he succeeded Mr. Witty at Cadeby and his place at Denaby

Charles Bury

was taken by Mr. Douglas Chambers. Outside his direct connection with the collieries, his principal interest in the life of the village was located on the cricket field. For ten years he captained a very strong Denaby and Cadeby cricket team in the Mexborough League, a position of which he was very proud, and which he held at the time of his death. Two years ago he had the satisfaction of leading the team to the championship. He was one of the most enthusiastic cricketers that were ever known. The very drudgery of long-fielding was a pleasure and delight to him. In the course of a match he would run three yards to any other fieldsman's one. He never attained any great proficiency apart from his capital fielding, and his record score in the League was forty-two, but his worth as a captain was considerable, and as a companion on a cricketing jaunt, inestimable.. He was a member of an old-established Barnsley family, of which his uncle, Mr. Reginald Bury, of the well-known firm of solicitors, is the present head.

Last Rites.
The last rites of the Roman Catholic Church were bestowed on the remains of this nonchalant but gallant hero of the mine on Tuesday afternoon, and there was again a great gathering of the village people to watch the progress of his body to it's last resting place. The little Catholic Church was quite crowded, and not the least sincere was the thick mass of colliers who stood at the back of the church and watched the last rites. The service was taken almost entirely in Latin, with all the ceremonial of

Charles Bury was born in Bombay in India and at the time of the 1911 Census he was living with his Aunt 55 year old Mary Agnes Bury and her companion 49 year old Lucy Maud Wootton. They had a Domestic Servant, 21 year old Mary Annie Nicholson.

John William Carlton
21 Tickhill Square, Denaby

The late J.W. Carlton, of 21 Tickhill Square, another of the mine heroes was laid to rest on Saturday afternoon at the Conisbrough Cemetery. Many friends were present at the funeral service, which was very impressive.

The Rev. F.S. Hawkes officiated. The coffin was supplied by Mr. G.L. Robinson, and made of oak, with the inscription :-John William Carlton, died July 9th 1912, Aged 38 years."

Principal mourners :- Mrs. Carlton and Mr. W. Page, Master J. Carlton and Miss C. Carlton, Mr. H. Carlton and Miss L. Carlton, Mr. J. Carlton (Lancs.), Mrs. Smith and Mr. J. Alexander, Mr. and Mrs. L. Damms, Mr. and Mrs. J. Alpine, Mr. and Mrs. H. Page, Mr. & Mrs. S. Page, Mr. & Mrs. T. Smith, Mr. J. Alpine & Miss S. Alpine, Master G. Alpine, Mr. H. Milner and Mrs. Smith. Bearers W. Golding, T. Gregory, T. Curtis, C. Biddolph, J. Brad, J. Higgins, C. Westby & T. Maddison.

John William Carlton originated from Middlestown in West Yorkshire and was married for 16 years to 40 year old Emma from Chesterton in Cambridgeshire. At the time of the 1911 census they had a daughter Clara aged 14 and a son John aged 12. A boarder John William Devlin aged 48 years, from Cumberland, was staying with them

John William Carlton's headstone
In Loving Memory of John William
The beloved husband of Emma Carlton
Who gave his life for others
In the Cadeby Colliery Disaster
July 9th 1912 aged 38 years
We cannot Lord thy purpose see
But all is well that's done by thee
Also their son Benjamin
Who died Aug 8th 1906 aged 10 months
"Safe in the arms of Jesus"

Arthur Carrol
38 Loversall Street, Denaby
Arthur Carrol was a 25 year old Dataller killed in the First Explosion.

Douglas Chambers
" Peveril " Conisbro'.

Another distinct loss is that of Mr. W.H. Chambers' young nephew, Douglas, who, after serving a pretty sound apprenticeship under Messrs. Thomsons, Manvers Main, and prior to that at Barrow Main was given the managership of Denaby Main a year ago,

while Mr. Charles Bury moved on to Cadeby Main. The appointment was looked upon as an experiment at the time, but the young man, who is only twenty-eight, justified himself at once, and was doing amazingly well when his career was cut short in this terrible fashion. With a few more years experience, most things would have been possible to Mr. Douglas Chambers. He was one of the men of the future. Eight or nine months ago he contracted a very happy marriage at Wincobank, and the grief of his young widow must be irrepressible.

Grim Evidence.

" At a cross-gate about eighty yards further on," the narrative went on, " we came across the rescue party named. They were apparently dead, with Mr. Bury the exception, but there was groaning from others in the group of victims who we did not know. Some of the party got Mr. Bury out and attended to him, we then came across Mr. Douglas Chambers. We thought there was a little life in him, and we set to work with energy trying to save him. But after trying artificial respiration for half an hour with oxygen there was no sign of life. All the victims of the disaster were interred amid all the manifestations of grief and respect which rightly belonged to the manner of their deaths, but Mr. Douglas Chambers, the clever young manager of the Denaby Main mine, who died while engaged in rescue work and was cut off in an instant by the second explosion, had the funeral obsequies of a distinguished hero. Nothing like it had been seen in Denaby since the funeral of Dr. Twigg, and even that impressive spectacle was outdone by reason of the infinitely more sombre setting

Impressive Spectacle

When Dr. Twigg was laid to rest the whole village mourned him, but now they were mourning not only Mr. Douglas Chambers, but eighty-six other brave men who died at their duty. The funeral service was timed for three o'clock, but in the mighty confusion which the disaster had produced, time-tables were as things of nought, and punctuality one of the most difficult of virtues. There was a great gathering in the neighbourhood of the dead manager's house, 'Peveril' in Elm Green Lane, but there were only two coaches leading the hearse containing the mortal remains of a young man who was just winning his way in the world and in the hearts of the people among whom he worked. The huge procession walked through the village to the church, and so on to the cemetery.

The hearse was preceded by the Denaby Main Ambulance Band, headed by Bandmaster, Mr. Moses Soar. Then came a long double-file of ambulance men, about one hundred and fifty of them all told, and then the coffin and the mourners. Behind the carriages came an open landau packed with wreaths, and behind that the long silent, bareheaded, procession of men representing the mining of South Yorkshire. There were colliery directors, mine managers, mine officials and colliers, all intermingling in one common sorrow, and there were also representatives of other institutions in which Mr. Douglas Chambers was interested.

The Ambulance Men.

Sergeant Parkinson, of the Wath Ambulance Division, of which Mr. Chambers was Superintendent, had pride of place among the ambulance men and prominent among them was Sergeant Winch, of the Wath Rescue Station, who narrowly escaped the second explosion, and made gallant efforts to save the poor fellows who were wiped out by it. Superintendent H.S. Witty led the ambulance party and marshalled the procession, and other Superintendents of Ambulance present were Mr. A.H. Barnard (Denaby), Mr. P. White (Mexborough), and Mr. H. Williamson (Melton), but they were in mufti, and took their places in the general ranks of the mourners.

A Deathly Hush.

Also appearing in the ranks of the ambulance men were Surgeon F.J. Burman of Wath, and J.J. Huey, of Mexborough, while Surgeon L. Ram of Swinton was also present amongst the mourners. Surgeons McArthur and Forster were at the time busy fighting for the life of Mr. Charles Bury, the other mine manager involved in the disaster.

From the main road opposite the little chapel, up to the churchyard railings and so on along to Tickhill Square, there must have been ten thousand people congregated to watch this heroic young man take his last journey, and the hush which fell on that great crowd as the cortege appeared 'in sight' to the strains of the slow measured accompaniment of the 'Dead March' in Saul, was one of the most impressive things I have yet encountered in a disaster in which nothing failed to impress.

The church, which is one of the most commodious in South Yorkshire, was well filled with mourners as the body was rested in the chancel, and the bearers :- Benjamin J. Hadfield, William Goodwin, Cyrus Schofield, A. Bond, Tom Allen, J. Buckle, and A. Dudhill (all Deputies), took their places in the choir-stalls. The Bishop of Sheffield, and his successor in the living of Doncaster, Canon Sandford, were stationed by the altar, and the Vicar of Denaby Main, the Rev, S.F. Hawkes, was at the prayer desk. Ranging back behind the chief mourners were men well-known in South Yorkshire mining.

Chief Mourners.

The chief mourners were :- Mr. J. Chambers, of Brampton Brierlow (father), Mr. W.H. Chambers, of The Dale, Conisbrough (uncle), Mr. J. Roper, of Darlington (uncle), Mr. Peter McGregor, of Sheffield (uncle), Mr. Willie Rope, of Dumfries (uncle), Mr. E.V. Rigg, of Cardiff, (brother-in-law), Mr. Herbert Ingold, of Wincobank, (uncle of the widow), Mr. Harry Radley and Mr. Sidney Radleyand and Mr. N. Mallinson , of Barnsley and Mr. Willie Nicholson, of Kircudbright, (uncle)

A Representative Assembly.

Among the public representatives who followed the last remains were :- J. Buckingham Pope (chairman of the Denaby and Cadeby Collieries), Captain M.E.W. Pope (director), Mr. Geo. Wilkie (secretary), Mr. R. Williamson (chief engineer), Mr. G.H. Ashwin (managing director Wath Main Collieries), Mr. A.F.T. Thomson (agent of the Manvers Main Collieries), Mr. W. Wilde (general manger of the Hickleton Main Collieries), Mr. C.W. Phillips (manager, Rossington Main Colliery), Capt. E.D.B. Johnson (Wath), Dr. G.H. Johnson (Wath), Dr. W.J. McClure (Conisbrough), Mr. G.H. Golightly (Sheffield), Councillor Clarke (Mayor of Doncaster), Mr. Frank Allen of Doncaster, Mr. W. Lowry Cole (agent to the Countess Marlborough), Mr. P.C. Bury, Mr. John Soar (under-manager Denaby Main), Mr. S.R. Johnson, Mr. J. Thompson and Mr. G. Williamson of Mexborough (representing the Denaby Lawn Tennis Club), Mr. S.J. Bridges, Mr. H.L. Smethurst, Mr. William Isaac Gibbs, Mr. Caleb Kilner J.P., Councillor J. Clayton (Mexborough), Mr. Arthur Dickenson (chairman Doncaster Licensed Victuallers' Asstn), Mr. J. Barlow, Mr. C Dodds, Mr. Steekins, Mr. A. Smalley, Mr. W. Venables, and many others.

After Canon Sandford had read a chapter from the Epistle to the Christians, the Bishop came down the chancel steps and addressed that big assembly of mourners.

The Bishop's Address.

The first words he spoke to them, he said, must of necessity be words of sympathy with those in that church who had been bereaved of those who were near and dear to them. "Only a few days ago," he continued, "all seemed smiling and happy. Work was good, wages were good, the weather was good, and altogether it seemed to be good. Then, all in a moment, a cloud descended upon us, and we are plunged today in the darkness of the shadow of death. For those who have lost their nearest and dearest our hearts beat, and go out to them in prayerful sympathy that God may succour them in their time of trial and trouble."

My next word must be of admiration and respect for the heroism which has characterised this terrible catastrophe. The silver lining of the cloud has been the heroism of the rescue parties who descended that fire-stricken mine, and tried to rescue those who were doomed. While we cherish admiration for the heroism of those who are dead, we also offer our respect for the heroism of those who were ready to die, and who are always ready to die for those who are perishing. Thinking as I do of the late Chief Inspector of Mines of this district, who is to be interred tomorrow at Doncaster, and whose body I saw only the other day with the medal of a hero lying on his breast given to him by the present King, I remember how he used say, " When I want a rescue party and call for volunteers, there are always three times as many offer as I can take down." One further word I would like to say. We cannot at this moment understand the mystery of this visitation. At the beginning of this week everything seemed to be inspiring and glorious. Our King and Queen have been in our midst, and we know how you value the sympathy of their Majesties. God moves in a mysterious way. That mystery will be revealed in the great day of revelations. " What I do thou knowest not how, but thou shalt know later. Oh satisfy us with Thy mercy, and that soon, so that we may apply our hearts unto wisdom. so that we may be glad and rejoice all the days of our life."

The Gathering Of A Storm.

The heat of mid-afternoon was sweltering, and as the great company of mourners moved slowly out of the church to the accompaniment of the sweetly, pathetic strains of Chopin's Funeral March, played by Mr. P. Green, the thunderclouds lowered and shortly the lightning flashed in great blue jagged streaks, adding the last touch of fitness to the scene. It seemed to be God's great natural illustration of what happened down that terrible mine ; the flash of flame and then the dull roar of the explosion. The band was silent now. Only the voice of the heavens could be heard, and at last the body of Douglas Chambers was committed to mother earth in a corner of the cemetery, the head of a long line of ominous looking trenches. It was very fitting that the manager should be buried with his men, as the dead captain on the field of slaughter.

The Widow's Tribute.

The coffin carried one bunch of lilies from the widow and parents of the poor fellow, but a continuous stream of floral tributes was passed along the line of ambulance men and placed around the open grave when the mourners had taken their last look. The coffin, which was of unpolished oak, was made by the brothers Robinson, who carried out the funeral arrangements, and it bore the simple inscription :- " Douglas Chambers, died July 9th, aged 28."

List Of Wreaths.

The wreaths, of which there were a large number, included a tall white cross inscribed,

" To our darling boy with God, from his father and mother," and the following : " To our dear boy, from his Auntie Annie and Uncle Willie (Nicholson) ; to a very dear nephew in loving memory, from uncle Jack and auntie Maggie (Roper) ; in loving memory of dear Douglas, a hero, from Mr. and Mrs. Brooke Willis ; a token of sympathy from the directors of Hickleton Main Colliery ; from all at the White House, Llandaff ; with deepest sympathy from the Wharncliffe Silkstone Colliery Co. ; from uncle Harry (W.H. Chambers) ; a token of regard from the Denaby Lawn Tennis Club, with sympathy sincere ; a token of respect from Mr. H. Guest, Ferry Farm ; maids of Broomfield, Sheffield ; from all at Darley, with sincere sympathy ; from the office staff at Cortonwood Colliery ; Fraulein Lothis, Bloomfield ; from the office staff and overmen at the Cortonwood Collieries, with deepest sympathy ; directors of Hickleton Main Colliery ; Capt. M.E.W. Pope ; Mr. J. Buckingham Pope ; in ever-loving memory of my first and oldest friend, from Hilda Pearson (Darlington) ; deepest sympathy from Denaby Main underground officials ; token of respect and sympathy from the overmen and deputies at Cortonwood and fondest thoughts from Ashley and George Longbotham ; Mr. and Mrs. Dayles' deepest sympathy ; Mr. William Clegg ; the teachers of Brampton Schools ; deepest sympathy from Brampton Cricket Club ; from the Wath Ambulance Corps, with many tokens of respect and sympathy from friends, which came too late to be classified.

The Storm Breaks.
The final notes of the stirring 'Last Post' had scarcely ceased quivering from the open grave when a terrible storm broke overhead, and torrential rain fell for half-an-hour, the storm being one of the fiercest known in Denaby for many years. The mourners at the funeral managed to reach shelter in time, but other mourners were less fortunate, particularly those at the funeral of Frederick J. Horsfall, a Sunday School teacher, who was included among the ill-fated deputies, and they had to brave the fury of the elements at the graveside. In consequence of the downpour the remainder of the funerals were considerably delayed, and the clergy did not conclude their sorrowful work until half-past eight in the evening.

Douglas Chambers' headstone
R.I.P. Douglas
Only beloved son of John Edwin and Helen Chambers
Died with rescue party In Cadeby Main
July 9th 1912, Aged 28 years

Robert William Chapman
7 Dufton's Row, Conisbrough

At the time of the 1911 Census Robert Willam Chapman was living with his wife, Elizabeth aged 30 from Cheltenham in Gloucester.They had been married for 3 years and had a 2 year old daughter, Edith who was born in Clifton.
Robert was listed as a Dayman Under Ground and originated from Leeds.

Headstone inscription:
In loving memory of Robert Willam,
the beloved husband of Elizabeth Chapman
who was accidentally killed in the Cadeby Mine Disaster July 9th 1912
aged 37 Years   Thy will be done
Also Winefred daughter of ...Who died Feb 1st 1913 Jesus called a little child ---

Thomas Cody
76 Clifton Street, Denaby Main

Funeral – Denaby Cemetery, Saturday.   Priest – Rev. Father Kavanagh.
Mourners :- Mrs. Cody (widow), Mr. Michael Managhan, Mr. Edward Managhan, Mr. T. Gilman, Miss Kate Cody (daughter), Mr. J. Gilman, Mr. W. Cross, Mr. J. Cross and Mr. Squire Pyne.
Bearers – Messrs. T. Higgins, E. Managhan, Michael Flynn, T. Doherty, T. Keary, M. Cody. A large number of miners attended the funeral.

At the time of the 1911 Cenus Thomas Cody was listed as a Carter, born in Manchester. He lived with his wife Margaret, aged 29 and from Motherwell.

They had 4 children: Mary Alice Cody, aged 10, John Cody, aged 6 and Thomas Cody, aged 3, all born in Manchester and Margaret Cody, aged 1, born in Middleton, Lancashire Also living with them was Thomas's mother, Mary Cody aged 79, a widowed, old aged pensioer, born in Longford in Ireland.

Eli Croxall
Tickhill Square, Denaby Main.
Story Of His Career. Public Interest In The Funeral.
The body of the late Mr. Eli Croxall, afternoon under-manager, was one of the last to

be recovered from the Cadeby mine, where, in common with so many other brave fellows, he met his death in the disastrous explosion of July 9th The large number of people that attended the funeral on Sunday evidenced the respect the deceased gentleman had gained during his working connection with the Cadeby Colliery and his residence at Denaby.

The late Mr. Croxall came to Cadeby in 1904, and was rightly appreciated as a thoroughly competent mining official. He had earlier gained valuable experience with the Walsall Wood Colliery Company Ltd. (Walsall Wood and Pelsall Collieries whose manager Mr. Arthur Hall), gave him the following good testimonial :- " This is to certify that I have known Mr. Eli Croxall for the last seven years. He has been my under-manager here during that time. He has been employed here by this company and the late Pelsall Coal and Iron Co. Ltd. for 24 years in the following capacities ;- Conductor – two years. Timberer – two years. Stallman – four years. Fireman – three years. Overman – two years, and Under-manger – eleven years. I have always found him to be a steady, honest, obliging, industrious and capable under-manager. He has had a great deal of experience in difficult seams with bad roofs, and also seven or eight years experience in electric coal-cutting. He is a thoroughly practical man and well-used to the handling of men, and I can well recommend him for a similar post to that which he has held here."

Eli Croxall

That is a tribute which speaks for itself. The truth of it all has received confirmation by the satisfactory service Mr. Croxall rendered to the Denaby and Cadeby Main Collieries Ltd. In the social movements of Denaby the deceased was a prominent figure. He resided in Tickhill Square, and was a main supporter of the cricket and bowling that have their home nearby.

The funeral took place on Sunday, and was conducted by the Rev. S.F. Hawkes (Vicar of Denaby), who held the first portion of the burial service in the Parish Church. The widow (Mrs. Croxall) was unable to attend through illness and her inability to leave her bed, to which she had been confined for three weeks.

The mourners included the following : Masters Clarence and Archie Croxall (sons), and Leslie Burley (nephew), of Doncaster, Mr. and Mrs. Trueman (sister and brother in-law), and Master B. Trueman, of Pelsall, Mrs. Burley (sister-in-law), of Doncaster, Mr. C. Mansfield (brother-in-law) of Bloxwich, Mr. and Mrs. R. Taylor (brother & sister-in-law), of Maltby, Mr. and Mrs. Fisher (cousins), of Wombwell, Mr. and Mrs. W. Lawrence, Mr. and Mrs. A. Taylor (brother& sister-in-law) of Maltby, Mr. and Mrs. J. Asher, Mr. McDonald, Mr. J. Dudhill and G. Fisher of Denaby, Mrs. Leader, of Doncaster.

The following deputies from the colliery acted as bearers :- Messrs. A. Sykes, G. Booth, T. Stones, A. Dudhill, J.H. Dudhill, E. Sheldon, J.J. Bucknell and T. Smith. Included in the large gathering of sympathising friends were :- Mr. H.S. Witty (the manager Cadeby Colliery), Mr. G.W. Robinson (underground – manager Manvers Main Colliery), Mr. Geo. Schofield (Mexborough), Mr. J. Winstanley (Mexborough), Mr. T. Springthorpe, Mr. H. Hinchliffe, and others. The coffin, which was of solid oak, with brass mountings, bore the inscription :- " Eli Croxall, Died July 9th 1912, aged 49 years." The scene at the Denaby Cemetery, as the Vicar uttered the committal sentences was a very impressive one. Some of the wreaths and flowers sent bore the following messages :- " To one we have loved and lost, from his sorrowing wife and children." " With love to dear Daddy, from Clarence and Archie." " In affectionate remembrance of our dear brother, from Mr. and Mrs. Trueman." There was also a wreath from Mr. and Mrs. Bateman (under-manager Shirebrook), and flowers from Mrs. Bucknall and Mrs. McDonald. bereavement.

Eli Croxall's headstone inscription:
Sacred to the memory of my dear husband Eli Croxall Aged 49 years
Whose life was lost in the Cadeby Colliery disaster July 9th
And whose remains were interred here 21st Sept 1912
In the midst of life we are in death   Also of his wife Clara Who died Aug 17th 1956

Herbert Cusworth
Cadeby Villas

Impressive Service At Hoyland.

The internment of the remains of Mr. Herbert Cusworth, who met with his death in the recent catastrophe at Cadeby, took place on Friday in the Tankersley Churchyard, in the presence of a large number of sympathising relatives and friends.

Deceased, who was the eldest son of Mr. and Mrs. Ezra Cusworth, of Beaumont Street, Hoyland Common, was an official at the Cadeby Colliery in the capacity of assistant under-manager, a position which he took up about Easter of last year. He had previously been in a similar position at the Hoyland Silkstone Colliery for about nine years, where, under his supervision, the new seam was opened out.

He had made rapid strides in the profession of his choice and bid fair to attain the topmost rung of the ladder in the mining world ; and the sudden ending of what promised to be a brilliant career, came as a great shock to a wide circle of friends. As an official he was held in high esteem by both men and master.

He was well-known in the cricketing world, both Tankersley with whom he played formerly, and Hoyland Silkstone, whose team he captained for several seasons, owing much of their success to his sterling ability. As a batsman he had few equals in the district, and his promotion to Cadeby signalised his inclusion into the Denaby team, with whom he played regularly in the Mexborough league matches.

Since the accident the suspense has been very trying, and the news of the recovery of his body, and only on Wednesday morning week, came as a great relief.

The deceased, who was in his thirty-seventh year, leaves a widow, and a family of three children, for whom, with his parents upon whom the blow has fallen heavily, the utmost sympathy is felt. Friday last, the day of the internment, was, by a strange coincidence, deceased's birthday, and had he lived he would have been thirty-eight years of age on that day.

The body was brought over from Cadeby in the afternoon, and as the sorrowful cortege left the home of the deceased's parents, genuine expressions of sympathy were heard on every hand. Hundreds of people lined the roadway.

The service in the church was as impressive a one as could be witnessed, and throughout there was a marked sense of the solemnity of the occasion. The service was conducted by the Rev. H.A. McNaughton, Rector of Tankersley, who, during the service gave a touching address, and the choir who were in full attendance sang with much feeling deceased's favourite hymns:-
" Jesus Lover of My Soul, " and " Nearer My God To Thee."

As the funeral cortege left the sacred edifice the " Dead March " in " Saul " was rendered on the organ by Mr. J. Burkinshaw. The committal service was also conducted by the Rev. H.A. McNaughton, and the choir sang, " Abide with me, Fast falls the eventide," another of deceased's favourite hymns.

William Charles Davis

Drabbles Yard, Conisbrough.

Funeral at Conisbrough Cemetery, on Sunday afternoon, the Rev. H. Rolfe, of the Baptist Connexion (Doncaster), being the officiating minister. The road en route was lined with people, and blinds were drawn as a last token of respect to one of Conisbrough's best-known athletes.

The Conisbrough United Brass Band headed the procession and played the "Dead March" in "Saul" in an impressive manner. Representatives from football clubs in Sheffield, Doncaster, Mexborough, Carcroft, Bentley and Silverwood attended. The Conisbrough St. Peter's F.C., with which deceased was intimately associated, was also represented, the president, treasurer, chairman and secretary being present.

Mourners :- Mrs. Davis (wife), Mr. and Mrs. Davis, Mrs. Ryan (grandmother), Elsie and Dorothy, Mr. and Mrs. C. Davis, Miss M. Davis, Mr. and Mrs. Byers (Birmingham), Annie, Doris and Percy Byers, Mr. and Mrs. W. Byers (Leeds), Mr. and Mrs. A. Halliday (Leeds).

The following members of the St. Peter's Football Club acted as bearers :- Messrs. C. Moseley, Yeomans, Butler, Harrison, Dawes, and Sheldrake. The wreaths were numerous and included a beautiful globe, subscribed for by the Football Club, and numerous floral tributes from relatives and friends.

" Conisbroite " writes :- " By his death, Conisbrough loses a well-known sports man, and above all a hero. The unfortunate young fellow lost his life in a brave attempt to save others. He had finished his own work in the mine and went back to help with the rescue work. He was asked to go out of the mine for refreshments, but declined, and so was entombed through the second explosion, and lost his life."

* * * *

The death occurred on Monday, at her residence, High Street, Conisbrough, of Mrs. Ryan, grandmother of William Davis, one of the victims of the Cadeby mine disaster. Death is believed to have been accelerated by the shock of her grandson's death. The deceased lady was well-known in the village.

George Royds Denton

42 Firbeck Street, Denaby

Funeral – Barnsley Cemetery, Saturday.   Priest – Rev. H. Mitchell officiating.
Mourners :- Mr. W. Royds (brother), Mr. T. Royds (brother), Mrs. Palmer (sister), Mrs. Corker (sister), Mrs. Lewis (sister). Wreaths from :-" Mr. and Mrs. Palmer," " Mr. Corker."

At the time of the 1911 census, George lived with his 26 year old brother, Thomas Willam Denton and his brother's wife 25 year old Amy Denton. Amy originated from Worksop and Thomas from Woodhouse. They had a 1 year old son John William Denton.

Also in the house was sister in law, 31 year old Susannah Johnson, and her children Albert Henry Johnson (2 months old) and Bertice Lilley aged 3 years.

William Dove
35 Gardens Lane, Conisbrough

Frederick Stone
39 Warmsworth Street, Denaby Main

Widow's Painful Disclosure At Inquest   A Painful Incident.
With the recovery of the last of the bodies remaining in the mine since the Cadeby Colliery disaster of July 9th last, the way was cleared for the final offices for the dead.

The prospects, so nearly realised, that in every case the remains would be identified, was unhappily frustrated at the last moment by the revelation of a sad mistake. The District Coroner, Mr. Frank Allen, and the standing jury met at the Colliery Surface offices on Saturday afternoon for the purpose of taking evidence of identification in connection with the last six bodies, and the proceedings were marked by an affecting scene. Two bodies could not be identified by the supposed widows and it appeared therefore, that their husbands had been buried under another name.

Mary Dove, of 27, Garden Lane, Conisbrough, said her husband, Willie Dove, aged 47, went to work the night before the explosion, and he had not been home since. She could not identify his body. Hannah Stone, a married woman, residing at 39 Warmsworth Street, Denaby, said her husband, Frederick Stone (33), was a collier, and went to work on the night previous to the explosion, returned home again, and afterwards went to the pit to join the rescuers. She had not seen him since, but had seen one of his boots in the colliery office.

Burial-Place Unknown.
The Coroner declared that under the circumstances it was impossible to tell where the two ladies' husbands were buried. They were buried somewhere in the parish and that was all he could say. But he would do his best to get them a proper certificate. There was no doubt that they both died on 9th July. If they once started trying to get to know where the two bodies really were, they would upset the feelings of other parties who had relatives buried.
Mr. W.I. Gibbs : Is it possible, Mr. Bridges, that he may have changed his boots ?
Mr. Bridges : Yes, sir. They have done that a lot.
Mrs. Stone : I think my husband changed his boots when he went down. The Coroner : Were there any boots found strewn about the pit, Mr. Bridges ?
Mr. Bridges : Yes, sir. A lot were picked up in the workings.
The Coroner : There have been more boots down there than feet to fill them.

Closing Burial Scenes. An Impressive Memorial Service.
The last burial service in connection with the Cadeby Colliery disaster was held at Denaby on Monday. In some respects it was more impressive than any of it's predecessors, in as much as the sorrowing mourners included the widows and relatives of two victims of the disaster, who had not been satisfactorily identified. In these sad circumstances, the services conducted in the Parish Church by the Vicar, had a special significance, for in the last rites the clergyman and the black-garbed congregation were gathered together for the purpose of committing to the ground " the poor earthly bodies of two men, who, by whatever name they were known in earthly life, had died nobly and bravely," and whose supposed widows were present humbly supplementing the prayers of the Vicar for their prayers of their souls to God. The widows in question were Mrs. Anna Stone, of 39 Warmsworth Street, Denaby Main, and Mrs. Mary Dove, of Gardens Lane, Conisbrough.
Before the cortege left the church the Vicar gave a short address relative to the unusual circumstances that surrounded them, and many of the congregation were moved to tears. The Vicar said : We have been asking week by week that the men and women should pray for those who have lost the men they have loved and they

have been praying. Now today we have an added sorrow. There is the doubt in the minds of those who are left whether they are really, this afternoon before the altar of God, with the bodies of those whom they loved. And therefore we want to ask ourselves what are we praying for this afternoon ? What are we doing ? We always do two things in a burial service. We commit the souls of those who have gone, to God's love and protection. We commit the dust to the dust whence it came. We are with no shadow of doubt and with absolute confidence gathered here this afternoon before the altar of God to commit to God's love and protection the souls of Frederick Stone and Willie Dove. We shall thank God in the church yard for taking the souls to himself. And what else are we doing ? We are committing the poor earthly bodies of two men, by whatever name we knew them in earthly life who died nobly and bravely – we are committing them to the earth with Christian reverence and Christian faith.

And lastly remember we have just said in the words of St. Paul, that the Father brought comfort to all Christian men and women from the days of our Lord and Master, who is himself the Resurrection and the Life. There is an earthly body and a spiritual body. Whatever doubt some may feel about the first there is none about the second. We are here committing the souls of Frederick Stone and Willie Dove to God's love and protection, knowing that he will clothe their souls in their spiritual bodies for their communion for all time in the hereafter with those who have loved them here on earth. So I ask your prayers. Ask God to comfort those who have who have had this trouble that he will make them ever thankful that they met together before his altar to commit the souls of their husbands to God's love and protection.

The united " Amen's " that followed the impressive utterance of the prayers made the atmosphere a spiritual one. At the cemetery the graves had been prepared in close proximity to each other, and the Vicar uttered the committal sentences in turn over each of the bodies.

The coffins bore the following inscriptions :-

" Presumed to be Willie Dove.   Who died 9th July 1912, aged 42 years."

and. " Presumed to be Frederick Stone,   Who died 9th July 1912, aged 33 years."

Arthur Dungworth

13 March Gate, Conisbrough

Arthur was buried in Conisbrough Cemetery at a funeral held by the Rev.C.P.Mellor. The mourners were his parents Mr and Mrs Dungworth, William, Tom and Harry, his brothers, Maria, Elizabeth, Elsie and Emma his sisters, Messrs A.Ackroyd and J.Tomlinson. The bearers were Messrs R.Ratcliffe, J.Smith, A.Hill, W.Nicholson, R.Kimberworth and J.Gelder.
A globe was sent by the workers union

The 1911 census, a year earlier, indicates that in the residence in March Gate lived 8 members of the family . His parents William, aged 55, Emma his wife aged 54 who had been married for 31 years. William was a plate layer at the Pit. His brothers William (28), driver at the pit, George (19), pit pony driver, Tom (13), brick carrier in Conisbrough and 12 year old Harry, not employed. Arthur's occupation was also listed as a Pit Pony driver at that time. The only sister living with them was 17 year old Emma

Robert Neil Eddington

Chapel Lane, Conisbrough. (Station Road, Conisbrough.)

Funeral – Conisbrough Cemetery, Friday.   Priest – Rev. W.A. Strawbridge.

Mourners :- Mr. J.M. Edington, Mrs. W. Edington (Manchester), Mr. Peterson (Manchester), Mrs. Hitchins (Manchester), Mr. and Mrs. Rigg (Manchester), Mr. J. Edington (Lancaster).

Wreaths from :- " Conisbrough Football Club," " Mr. and Mrs. Rigg," " Mr. and Mrs. Wm. Edington (Manchester)," " Mr. J. Edington," " Mr. and Mrs. Ibbeson (Conisbrough)."

Sydney Ellis
49 Holywell Road, Conisbrough

FUNERAL OF MR. S. ELLIS, A popular Official

The funeral of Mr. Sydney Ellis, one of the victims of the Cadeby disaster, whose body was but recovered last week end, took place at Denaby on Monday, the Rev. S.F. Hawkes officiating.

He was but 32 years of age, and had been married about three years.

The scenes attending these last sad rites were very impressive, a large crowd gathering to witness the conveyance of the cortege and also at the graveside.

There was a large attendance of mourners, and many beautiful floral tributes were sent.

He was a highly promising young surveyor ands highly popular with all who knew him in Conisbrough and Denaby

His body was borne to the grave by members of the Conisbrough Cricket Club, namely Messrs. D. Graham, W. Oxley, F. Butler and W. Appleyard, with about thirty members of the cricket club walking in procession.

Previous to coming to Conisbrough, Mr. Ellis was a member of the Doncaster Parish Church choir, and up to the time of his death was a valued member of the Denaby Church choir.

He was 3rd officer in the local Ambulance Corps., and was captain of the Conisbrough cricket team playing in the South Yorkshire league.

MR. SIDNEY ELLIS.
One of the Cadeby Explosion Victims. He was the younger son of the late Councillor E. Ellis, of Doncaster.
Mr. Ellis was a scholar at the Oxford Place Wesleyan School, Doncaster, and was for some time a member of the Doncaster Parish Church Choir. He was a very promising young surveyor, and highly popular with all who knew him both at Conisborough and Denaby.

Phillip George Evans
68 Annerley Street, Denaby Main.

Funeral – Denaby Cemetery, Friday.
Mourners :- Mrs. Evans (widow), Mr. Frank Evans, Mr. and Mrs, Bates, Mr. and Mrs. M. Evans, Mr. H. Pearson and Miss Evans, Lily, Elsie and Isaac Evans, Mr. and Mrs. M. Pearson, Mr. and Mrs. P. Pearson, Mr. and Mrs. Lily.
Floral tributes were sent by :-" Mrs. Wren," " Mr. and Mrs. Pearson," " Mr. and Mrs. Lily and their Son Frank."
Bearers – Messrs. Higgins, Davy, Wren, Hartley, Beckett, Worsley, Beckett, Cocker, Bradley and Kavanagh.

Thomas Emrys Evans
Wales.

A Broken-Hearted Father.
One of the most pathetic figures among those who have wearily waited for news at the colliery has been that of a Congregational minister of Penarth, the father of Emrhys Evans, a mining student, who is still locked up down the mine. He has hung about for some days in the desperate hope of the news that could not be given him, and has aroused the sympathy of all by his evident distress.

A Cadeby Hero.
Memorial To Be Erected To Manchester Scholar.
An echo of the Cadeby pit disaster was heard at the Manchester Grammar School Speech Day, on Wednesday, when Mr. Paton, Highmaster, told a thrilling story of the heroism of Emrys Evans, an old scholar.

Evans, he said, was a mining student visiting Denaby, when his landlady, at breakfast, told him of the explosion. He asked for his pick and his pit-suit, hurried to the scene of the disaster, and was one of the first volunteers to join the rescue party which perished. They were proud of him, and intended to place a memorial in the school

Supplied by Rachel Kneale, Archivist, Manchester Grammar School from the school magazine (Ulula) :
T. Emrys Evans lost his life in the fatal colliery accident at Cadeby on Tuesday July 9th. He was the eldest son of the Rev. Jonathan Evans, Minister of Milton Church, Rochdale. He entered the school in 1904. After leaving us, he took a course in Mining Engineering, and had arranged during his holiday to visit certain mines in the Conisborough district with a view to acquiring practical experience. He selected the Denaby Collieries because of the reputation they had for the efficiency of their general arrangements. He was going to sit for his final examination next March.

He arrived at Conisborough on the evening of Monday, July 8th. On going to bed, he told his landlady not to call him till 7 o'clock as it was not his intention to go down the pit the following day. The King and Queen were visiting the district and he proposed to see them. At breakfast his landlady told him of the catastrophe. He got up at once, took his bag with his pit suit, went off to the pit, and was among the first to volunteer. While the rescuers were down the pit at work, the second explosion took place, even more deadly than the first, and

Evans with nearly all the rescue party was buried beneath masses of fallen material.

The Grammar School is proud of her son. When duty called, he was not wanting. He played the man in the face of danger, and gave his own life to save the lives of others. As he was in death, so he was in life; always unselfish, always willing to help, strong in body and in will, singularly high-minded and pure.

Many old boys will remember his younger brother, the gallant young soul, Mervyn Evans, who died on the football field in a match against the Rochdale Rugby Football Club. The sympathy of all who knew them will go out towards the parents who taught their lads to be brave men.

A subsequent edition of the magazine reports:
The body of Emrys Evans was recovered on September 21st; it had been 73 days entombed in Cadeby mine. He was found beside a young inspector called Lewis; they seem to have been engaged in rescuing the bodies of two colliers who were killed by the first explosion.

The inquest was held immediately after the body was brought up, and the funeral was held at Penarth on Tuesday, September 24th. The High Master with a few

Thomas Emrys Evans Memorial

friends met the body when it was brought into Sheffield and a wreath was laid on the coffin in the name of his Old School. Steps are being taken to put up a memorial tablet to his memory in the School building. The Governors have given their sanction, and the matter will be laid before the next meeting of the O.M.A. executive.

Thomas Fleck
8 Holywell Street, Conisbrough

Funeral – Conisbrough Cemetery, Saturday. Priest – Rev. E. Grieves (Wesleyan)

Mourners : Mrs. Simpson and Mrs. Robson (Northumberland), Miss Annie Blackburn, Mr. and Mrs. Blackburn, Miss N. Blackburn, Mr. J. Baines (Rotherham Mr. and Mrs. Snow (Doncaster), Mr. and Mrs. Fletcher (Doncaster), four 'chums' from the Doncaster Football Club, Mrs. Oddy and daughters, Messrs. J. Hall and W. Oddy.

The Conisbrough Wesleyan Mission Band attended.
Bearers – His four friends from the Doncaster Football Club.
Wreaths :- From his Football Chums."

Charles William Fletcher
47 Maltby Street, Denaby Main

At the time of the Census in 1911, Charles William Fletcher lived with his wife of 6 years, 28 year old Mary Fletcher. Both came from Horbury in West Yorkshire.

They had a 3 year old daughter, Ivy Fletcher, born in Denaby Main.

John Fletcher
40 Edlington Street, Denaby Main

.

Funeral – Denaby Cemetery, Friday.   The Rev. S.F. Hawkes officiating.
Mourners :- Mr. Thomas Soar (stepson), Mrs. E. Fletcher (widow), Mr. Wm. Osborne (stepson), Mrs. Mannion (sister-in-law), Mr. Brammah, Mr. and Mrs. J. Brett.
Wreath from :- " Mrs. Jackson."

At the time of the Census in 1911, John Fletcher lived with his wife of 19 years, Elizabeth, aged 53 years and from Heanor in Derbyshire.

Also living with them was their Son in law William Osborne, aged 33, a marine store dealer, also from Heanor. John Fletcher came from Langley in Derbyshire

Arthur Flynn
109 Tickhill Street, Denaby Main

The funeral of Arthur Flynn, one of the victims of the Cadeby explosion took place at Denaby cemetery on July 13th.

The chief mourners were :- Mr. and Mrs. J. Flynn (father and mother), Mrs. C. Finn, Misses M. Flynn, A. Flynn, E. Flynn, C. Flynn, Tom and Pat, Maggie Flynn (brothers and sisters), Mr. and Mrs. Dunhill, Mrs. Newall, Mr. and Mrs. Lindsay, Mr. C. Finn, Mr. and Mrs. Jones (Denaby), a large number of his fellow work mates and friends, while the National Irish Foresters acted as bearers.

Wreaths and flowers were sent from :-
Father, Mother, Aunt Frances. (Anchor). Aunt Sarah (Cross), Uncle Jack (Cross).
Wreath from Don. W.M. Club (Mexborough).

Flowers from Miss Violet Cocker (Mexborough), and from his sisters and brothers.

At the time of the 1911 Census Arthur lived with 14 other people at 92 Cliff View, Denaby Main

Name:	Relation	Sex:	Age	Occupation:	Where born:
Flynn, John	Head	M	41	Coal Miner Hewer	Doncaster
Flynn, Martha J.	Wife, 19 Years	F	36		Doncaster
Flynn, Arthur	**Son**	**M**	**19**	**Pony Driver Pit**	**Doncaster**
Flynn, Mary F	Daughter	F	17	Sewing Maid	Doncaster
Flynn, Martha	Daughter	F	15		Doncaster
Flynn, Elizabeth	Daughter	F	14		Doncaster
Flynn, Annie	Daughter	F	12	School	Denaby
Flynn, Catherine	Daughter	F	9	School	Denaby
Flynn, Thomas	Son	M	8	School	Denaby
Flynn, Patrick	Son	M	7	School	Denaby
Flynn, Margaret	Son	F	4		Denaby
Flynn, Winifred	Daughter	F	1		Denaby
Flynn, Sarah	Daughter	F	1 Mnth		Denaby
Finn, Charles	Boarder	M	29	Coal Miner Hewer	Caracastle, Irelnd
Pearce, William	Boarder	M	21	Coal Filler	Skegby

Joseph Benjamin Fox

66 Earnshaw Lane, Conisbrough

Funeral Conisbrough Cemetery, Friday 12th July; Priest; Rev. C.P.Mellor.
Mourners: Mr. and Mrs. B.Fox (father and mother), Alice and Ernest, Abraham and Minnie, Mr. and Mrs Swan (Walsall Wood, Staffs), Mr. and Mrs.Hinton, Denaby, Mr. and Mrs. J.Fox, Mr,C.Senior and Miss E.Hinton, Mr.A,Addy, Mrs W.Birch, George and Nellie Orgill, Mrs Cunningham and Mrs. Butler. Messsrs. Verity, Smith, Feirn and Walker. Bearers: Messrs C.Largon, J.Brammer, E.Hague, J.Hinton, C.Senior and E.Hemsall. Wreaths: From "Father & Mother" "Sisters and brothers" " friends at Clifton

At the time of the 1911 Census, Joseph Benjamin, born in Pelsall in Staffs, lived with his parents at Clifton. The head of the household, Benjamin Fox aged 42, was a Coal Hewer from Walsall in Staffs; his wife Mary Ann was 56 and they had been married for 24 years. Also in the house were brothers Ernest, aged 19 and also a Pony Driver, and Abraham aged 16, a lamp carrier below ground. The other occupant was their sister Minnie aged 12.

William Frankland

5 Rowena Row, Conisbrough

Funeral Conisbrough Cemetery, Saturday 13th July   Minister – Rev. H. Rolfe (Baptist)
Mourners :- Mrs. Frankland (widow), Mr. T. Frankland (brother)(Featherstone), Mrs. Newby (sister) (Heckmondwike), Mrs. Fisher (sister) (Heckmondwike), Mrs. T. Frankland (sister-in-law) (Featherstone), Miss Noble (niece), Mr. W. Banks (brother-in-law) (Conisbrough), Miss Dove (niece) (Conisbrough), Mr. and Mrs. Newby (Heckmondwike), Mr. P. Parkinson, Miss Midgeley, Mr. F. Midgeley, Mr. and Mrs. Dutton, Mr. and Mrs. Cockroft (Bradford), Mrs. C. Parkin and Mrs. Sykes (Heckmondwike), Mr. and Mrs. A. Dove (Conisbrough), Mr. and Mrs. Wood (Denaby), Mr. and Mrs. Jenkinson (Conisbrough), Mr. Tomkimson, Mr. E. Dove (Liversedge), Mr. D. Jones (Conisbrough). Wreaths :- " From Wife and Daughter," " Tom Frankland," " Mr. Douglas O. Jones," and others.

Richard Gascoyne

78 Loversall Street

At the time of the Census, Richard Gascoyne lived with his family in Loversall Street:

Person	Relation	Sex:	Age	Occupation:	Where Born:
Gascoyne, Osric	Head	M	43	Coalminer, Hewer	Heanor, Derbys
Gascoyne, Sarah	Wife, 23 Years	F	40		Ridding, Derbys
Gascoyne, Richard	**Son**	**M**	**21**	**Pony Driver, Colliery**	**Somercoates, Derbys**
Gascoyne, Ann Eliz	Daughter	F	19		Hemsworth
Gascoyne, Lucy	Daughter	F	17		Cudworth
Gascoyne, Clara E	Daughter	F	16		Heanor, Derbys
Gascoyne, Joseph	Son	M	14	Door Trapper	Heanor, Derbys
Gascoyne, Alice	Daughter	F	12	School	Mexborough
Gascoyne, Osric	Son	M	11	School	Mexborough
Gascoyne, Walter	Son	M	5	School	Denaby Main
Gascoyne, Rose	Daughter	F	2		Denaby Main
Gascoyne, Beatrice	Daughter	F	5 Mnths		Denaby Main
Cooper, Samuel	Widower	M	54	Coalminer, Hewer	Whitwick, Leics

William H. Godsmark

65 Lime Grove, Conisbrough

William Godsmark was a 28 year old dataller. His body was recovered from the Pit on 10th September, 1912

William Green

9 Marr Street, Denaby Main

William Green was born in Staffordshire in 1886, he moved to Denaby about 1908 looking for work. William was married to Elizabeth before the move.

At the time of the Cadeby Pit Explosion they had 2 girls Carrie born 1908 and Florence born 1910. Wilhelmina was born on 30th August 1912 and married Harry Higgins, the second son of a miner in 1933.

The husband of her daughter, Brian Hobson from Christchurch in Dorset has kindly supplied the photos of William Green and (below) the wedding of Wilhelmina to Harry Higgins. Elizabeth Green is seated second from the left.

Tobias Hancock

2 Yew Terrace, Conisbrough

At the Census in 1911 Tobias Hancock was lodging with William and Anne Tummins at 2 Yew Terrace.
Also in the house were 4 Chadwick brothers; Sam, 21years, Harold 14 years, Joe 16years and Jim 13 years old.

Michael Hayden
77 Firbeck Street, DenabyMain

Funeral – Denaby Catholic Cemetery, Friday, 12th July, 1912
Priest – Rev. Father Kavanagh officiating
Mourners :- Mr. Arthur Hayden (son), Mr. F. Hayden (brother), Mr. P. Neath (cousin),
Mrs. Whitworth, Mr. John Robinson, Mr. Ernest Harcroft, Mr. John Driscoll.

Edward Henderson
65 Balby Street, Denaby Main

Funeral – Denaby Cemetery, Friday 12th July,1912 Priest – Rev. S.F. Hawkes and Rev.
J.W.Tunnicliffe.

Mourners :-Mrs. Henderson (widow), Mrs. Dady (sister), Mr. E. Henderson (son), Mr.Ernest
Henderson (son), Miss May Henderson (daughter), Mrs. Boyland (mother), Mr Royston, Mr.
Boyland (son), Miss F. Boyland, Miss M. Boyland, Mr. W. Boyland, Mr. A. Boyland, Mr. C.
Boyland, Mr. Vincent Boyland, Mr. Wilfred Boyland, Mr. Thomas Boyland, Mr. Marshall,
Mr. and Mrs. Ellis, Mr. and Mrs. Myers, Mr. and Mrs. Timmins, Miss Smallbridge, Mrs.
Jenkinson, Mrs. Waring.

Bearers – Messrs. Kitchen, Riley, F. Royston, W. Royston, T. Royston, Butcher and T.W.
Kitchen. Wreaths from :-" Mrs. Waring,"" Mr. and Mrs. Hurst," and" Mr. Waring (Kinsley)."

*At the time of the Census John Henderson lived with his wife of 11 years, Edith, aged 31.
Also in the house at 65 Balby Street were sons, Edmund, Ernest and Harold aged 10 years,
8 years and 1 year respectively. Also daughter May aged 4 years.*

Edith came from Chapeltown and all the family were born in Denaby.

George Heptinstall
85 Clifton Street, Denaby Main

*George Heptinstall was a Corporal in the Mine and at the 1911 Census lived with his wife of
8 years, Eva, aged 28 at 85 Clifton Stret. They both originated from Gawthorpe in Yorkshire.*

*Also living with them was their 4 year old daughter Doris and 1 year old son William. Both
Children were born in Batley Carr in Yorkshire.*

George Heptinstall's headstone Inscription:

In loving memory of George
The beloved husband of Eva Heptinstall
Who lost his life with the rescue party
In the Colliery disaster at Cadeby Main
July 9th 1912 aged 28 years
Greater love hath no man than this
That he lay down his life for his friend

Letter from Shirley Clements:

George Heptinstall was my maternal grandfather, born in Gawthorpe, Ossett, on the 23rd September 1883. He was the eldest son of William Heptinstall and his wife Emily (formerly Eastwood and born in Swinton/Mexborough). In the late 1880's he moved to Batley, where he lived with his parents, brothers James and Willie and sister Mary Ann. In 1901 he was working as a "carter".

George married Emily Eva Fozard (born 1882 in Gawthorpe, Ossett) at All Saints' Parish Church, Batley, on the 25th July 1903 (see wedding photograph). The name on the marriage certificate was George Marshall Heptinstall, in memory of his grandmother Elizabeth Heptinstall (formerly Marshall) who had died in April of that year. His occupation was recorded as "teamer". Four of George and Eva's six children were born in the Batley/Batley Carr area: Elsie (1904), Doris (my mother, 1906), Emily (1908) and William (1909). Elsie and Emily died in infancy.

George and his family moved to Denaby Main between July 1909 and April 1911, possibly because of his mother's link to this area. At the time of the 1911 Census, George was a corporal, aged 27, working below ground in the coal mine. He lived at 85 Clifton Street with his wife Eva (aged 28), daughter Doris (aged 4) and son William (aged 1). In June 1911 another daughter (Evelyn) was born but she survived only 25 days.

The records indicate that George was killed in the second explosion that occurred at the Cadeby Main Colliery on July 9th 1912. The cause of death was "afterdamp". My mother Doris always told me that her father had survived the first explosion but had gone back into the mine to rescue the trapped miners and had died in the second explosion. He was buried on the 13hJuly in the cemetery of All Saints' Parish Church, Denaby.

George's tragic death had a big impact on family life. Only one month after George died, Eva gave birth to another daughter, Ivy, and the children were separated. William, aged 3, remained in Denaby Main with Eva and baby Ivy, but my mother Doris, aged 6, was sent to Batley to live with her grandmother, Emily Heptinstall, and never lived with Eva again.

Eva remarried twice and lived in Denaby Main for many years. She had another six children but five died in infancy. George and Eva's youngest daughter Ivy and a stepbrother died on the same day in the flu epidemic of 1919. I can't imagine how my grandmother Eva coped with all the tragedy that she faced: she died in Doncaster in 1939, aged 57, before I was born. My mother Doris and her brother William were the only children of George and Eva to survive into adulthood. William developed multiple sclerosis, never married and died aged 74 in 1983. My mother died in 2001, aged 95.

Unfortunately, it was only after my mother's death that I found out about the Miners Chapel at All Saints' Church and in 2007 the Vicar very kindly opened the Church and showed me around. It was a very emotional experience and I wish that my mother had been there. I am the only grandchild of George and Eva Heptinstall and my grandfather's bravery will be remembered always by me and my family.

Henry Richard Hewitt
Sheffield

The loss of Mr. Henry Richard Hewitt, who was among the three Government Inspectors who were killed, will be keenly felt in mining circles.

Mr. Hewitt, who was forty-six years of age, was born at Swannick, near Alfreton, and was the son of the late Mr. John Richardson Hewitt, M.I.C.E. In the month of March 1911, he took up his residence in Sheffield, on being promoted to the senior inspectorship of the Yorkshire district.

Mr. Hewitt leaves a widow and two young children

Below are the 4 Mine Inspectors involved: Mr. G.Y.Tickle, Doncaster (killed), Mr Wilson, Leeds (who escaped death), Mr.W.H.Pickering (killed), Mr H.R.Hewitt, Sheffield (kiled)

George Hindson
Cadeby Village

Mexborough Times, September 12th
THE CADEBY DISASTER.
Mine Giving Up It's Dead.
Four More Bodies Recovered.

The delicate and drawn out task, so capably undertaken by the rescue parties in the Cadeby mine, is now within sight of completion. This week four more bodies have been recovered. The first of the four brought to the surface was that of Mr Herbert Cusworth (39), afternoon under-manager, of Cadeby Villas, Conisbrough, whose remains were recovered on Wednesday.

The following night three more of the victims were removed to the pit-top. On Thursday the remains of one were identified as those of George Hindson (25), dataller, of Cadeby Village. Conisbrough

Frederick William Horsfall

149 Tickhill Street

The funeral of the late Mr. F.W. Horsfall, assistant surveyor of the Cadeby Colliery, and one of the heroes of the recent colliery disaster, took place on Friday 12th July at the Denaby Cemetery. Mr. Horsfall was known by all and held in high esteem. He will be much missed in the village, having been in the parish church since the age of seven, and a Sunday-school teacher in the schools. He was well connected with the St. John Ambulance Brigade, holding prizes which he won in 1906. He was a member of the cricket club, the C.E.M.S., the Institute Mining class, and a most zealous church worker.

The funeral service, which was held in the Parish Church, was fully choral, and was conducted by the Rev. F.S. Hawkes and W.J.W. Tunnicliffe. The choir sang the 34th and 90th Psalms and hymn, " On the resurrection morning."

The coffin was borne from the church to it's last resting place by members of the Ambulance Brigade, followed by a retinue of members and nursing sisters, under the able command of Superintendent H. Williamson.

Then came the chief mourners, which included :- Mr. and Mrs. J. Horsfall, Miss May Horsfall, Mr. and Mrs. W. Wathey, Mr. and Mrs. E. Wathey, Mr. and Mrs. F. Wathey, Mr. and Mrs. A. Perry, Miss E. Wathey, Miss H. Jones, Mrs. W. Wathey (South Kirkby), Mr. Haywood (Sheffield), Mr. T. Shrives, Mrs. Cook, Mr. and Mrs. E. White, Mr. and Mrs. H. Wathey, Mrs. Tyler (Ilkeston), Mr. A. Jones, Mr. H. White, Mrs. R. Middleton (Sheffield), Miss F. Smith, Miss B. Bennett, and about thirty friends.

William Humphries

29 Tickhill Square, Denaby Main

The funeral of Mr. W. Humphries, the highly respected deputy of the Cadeby Colliery, and hero and victim of the great disaster, took place on Sunday afternoon 22nd September at Mexborough Cemetery.

Deep sympathy was shown on all sides, and every respect was paid to a good workmate and comrade. A squad from the Denaby St. John Ambulance Division were in attendance under the superintendence of Captain H.S. Witty and Sergeant Major Power. The Nursing Division (of which Mrs. Humphries is a member, and to whom she is indebted for their many kindnesses) were represented by :-Mrs. Yates, Mrs. Ellsey, Mrs. Hilton, and Mrs. Cavanagh.

Members of the rescue party and ambulance brigade acted as bearers. The chief mourners were : Mrs. Humphries, Mr. S. Humphries, Cissie and Austin Humphries, Mrs Humphries, Mrs Laycock, Mr. and Mrs. H. Humphries, Mr. and Mrs. W. Humphries, Mr. and Mrs. P. Humphries, Mr. and Mrs. Tilson, Mr. and Mrs. S. Tilson, Mr. J. Tilson, Mr. and Mrs. W. Hammond, Mr. and Mrs. Hathaway, Willie and Tom Tilson, Miss Tilson, Miss Epplestone, Mr. and Mrs. G. Tilson, Mr. and Mrs. Sidebottom, Mr. and Mrs. Littlewood, Mr.

and Mrs. A. Lawley, Mrs. Horsfall, Mrs. Wilkinson, and many other relatives and friends. The coffin was of plain oak, and bore the inscription :-" William Humphries, Died July 9th 1912, aged 33 years." Mr. G.L. Robinson carried out the whole of the funeral arrangements.

Many wreaths and crosses were received, amongst which were seen those from :- " His sorrowing Wife and Children.", " Father and Mother.", " Members of the Rescue Party."" Mr. and Mrs. Littlewood." " Mr. and Mrs. Horsfall,", " Mr. and Mrs. Wilkinson," " Uncle and Aunt.(Barnsley)."" Relatives at Bromley." " Mr. and Mrs. W. Humphries.", " Mr. Scannon and Miss Best." and flowers from " Phoebe," Mrs. Hulley, Mrs. Tilson, Mrs. Engledow, Mrs. Brazier, and many others. The carriages were supplied by Mr. J.H. White, Mexborough.

Charles Albert Hunt
97 Clifton Street, Denaby Main

A Military Funeral.
Perhaps one of the most impressive spectacles of Saturday, 13th July was the funeral of Charles Hunt, who was interred at Conisbrough Cemetery with military honours, being a member of the local detachment of the Territorial Army.

The Territorials, to the number of seventy, including the bugle band, followed the bier to the cemetery to the solemn strains of the 'Dead March'. Rev. W.A. Strawbridge officiated.
Mourners :- Mrs. Hunt (widow), Elsie and Dolly Hunt (daughters), Mr. and Mrs. Dungworth, Mr. and Mrs. Ackson, Mrs. Hynes (mother), Mrs. Peck (sister), Mrs. Troughton, Mr. Troughton, Mr. W. Dungworth, Mr. G. Dungworth, Mrs. Hill, Mrs. Church, Mr. F. Staniforth, Mr. J.R. Bowling, Miss Alice Bell.

Bearers – (Denaby Territorials) Lance-Corporal E. Davis, Corporal H. Palmer, Pte. J. Bentley, Pte. R. Redpath, Pte. W. Brookes, and Pte. J. Showell.

Wreaths :-" From the Officers commanding 'G'. Company," " the N.C.O's. of 'G' Company Territorials,"" Father and Mother," " Widow and Children," and " Mr. and Mrs. Hunt (Birmingham)."

Samuel George Jackson
102 Doncaster Road, Denaby Main

Last weekend the rescue party were successful in extricating another body from the Cadeby mine. It was identified later by Mr. J. Jackson as that of his brother, Mr. Samuel Jackson, assistant deputy, of Doncaster Road.

The funeral took place on Tuesday, 27th August at the Mexborough Cemetery, amidst scenes of deep sympathy. The remains were enclosed in a plain oak coffin with brass mountings, and bore the inscription : " Samuel George Jackson Died July 9th 1912, aged 30 years."

The officiating bearers were Messrs. T. Smith, E. Kelly, B. Shaw, J. Illingworth, R. Winfield, C. Senior, W. Marshall, and J. Dudhill.
The chief mourners were :- Mrs. Jackson (widow), Mr. J. Jackson, Mr. A. Jackson, Louise and Albert Jackson, Mrs. Porter, Misses C. Dodd and H. Cartwright, Mrs. Windle and

Miss L. Jackson, Mr. and Mrs. Cartwright, Mr. and Mrs. Dodd, Miss Froggatt and Mr. Windle, Mr. Porter, Miss G. Cartwright, Mr. and Mrs. Beston, Mr. and Mrs. Oakley, Mr. and Mrs. Hall, Mr. J. Windle, Mr. Rodway, Mr. and Mrs. Asher Mr. and Mrs. Butterfield, Mr. and Mrs. Chetwynd, Mrs. Dudhill, Mrs. Constantine, Mrs. Dutton, Mrs. Kelsall, Mrs. Marshall, Mrs. Shaw, Mrs. Deakin, Mrs. Addshead.

The Rev. S.F. Hawkes performed the last solemn rites, and Mr. G.L. Robinson carried out the funeral arrangements.

Charles Johnson (Died in Hospital)
78 Cliff View, Denaby Main

At the 1911 Census Charles Johnson lived with his wife of 13 years, Sarah aged 37 from Dudley. They had 6 children all born in Dudley; Beatrice aged 12, Gladys aged 10, Samuel aged 8, Walter aged 7, Mat aged 4 and Ivy aged 1.

Matthew Jordan
61 Loversall Street, Denaby Main

Matthew Jordan was buried on 13th July, with Minister Tunnicliffe officiating. He was aged 52 and died in the First Explosion.

John William Kelsall

66 Ravenfield Street, Denaby Main

The funeral of the late G.W. Kelsall, assistant deputy of the Cadeby Colliery, and a hero in the recent disaster, took place on Friday, 12th July at Denaby cemetery. Only a young man, yet he held the esteem of all his fellow workmen and those with whom he came into daily contact.

Mr. G. Robinson supplied the coffin which was borne by Messrs. J. Roberts, B. Roberts, W. Soar, T. Deringham, J. Davis and T. Chambers. The funeral service was by the Rev. F.S.Hawkes, assisted by Rev. J.W Tunnicliffe.

The principal mourners included :- Mrs. Kelsall (widow), Mr. and Mrs. J. Kelsall, Mrs. Dunning, Mr. J. Kelsall jnr., Masters F.& H. Kelsall, Mr. and Mrs. Wood, Mrs. James, Mr. and Mrs. Flinders, Mr. and Mrs. W.H. Dunning, Mr. S. Dunning, Mr. and Mrs. T. Soar, Mrs. Hewitt, Miss L. Dunning, Mr. and Mrs. Bowes, Mr. W. Hynes, Mrs. Lumb, Mrs. Ellis, Mr. A. Sidway, Mr. and Mrs. Cheshire, Mr. and Mrs. Taylor, Mr. H. Perry, Mr. Littler, Mr. and Mrs. Kelsall, Mr. R. Kelsall, and Mr. F. Kelsall.

John William Kelsall, from Smalltorne in Staffordshire had been married 2 years to Denaby born Florence, aged 20 at the time of the census. They had an 11 month old daughter Edna

William Lambert
75 Loversall Street, Denaby Main

Sarah Ann Lambert, William's wife, was also aged 29 and came from Misterton. They had 4 children at the 1911 census; George Herbert aged 8 born at Barnby Dun, Ivy aged 5 born in Misterton, Minnie aged 3 and Elsie aged 1 both born locally.

William originated from Feller Thorne in North Yorkshire

Gravestone inscription
In loving memory of Willam,
the beloved husband of Sarah Ann Lambert
who gave his life for others
in the Cadeby Colliery Disaster, July 9th 1912,
Aged 29 Years
Greater Love hath no man

John Marrow (alias Marsden)
62 Loversall Street, Denaby Main

The funeral took place on Friday of John Marrow, who was accidentally killed in the Cadeby Colliery Explosion, at St. Margaret's Church, Swinton, from his mother's residence, 52 York Street, Mexborough.

Deceased was well-known and highly respected in the surrounding district. He leaves a widow and family of two sons to mourn his loss.

Mourners were :- Mrs. Marrow (widow), Mathew and Colin (sons), Mr. Harry Marrow (brother), Mrs. Marrow (mother), Mr. Wilfred Marrow, brother, Mr. Tom Marrow and Mrs. Senior (brother and sister), Mr. Colin Marrow and Mrs. Brownhill (brother and sister), Mr. Brownhill and Mr. Wm. Senior (brothers-in-law), Mr. and Mrs. Bentley, Mr. and Mrs. P. Bentley, Mrs. Wilfred Marrow, Mr. and Mrs. Rowlands, Mr. and Mrs. Birch, Mr. and Mrs. Alf Bentley, Mr. Hackney, Mr. H. Bentley, Mrs. A. Gibson, Miss Barber, Misses Phyllis and Mary Ann Wilkinson, Miss Nora Senior, Mr. Wm. Senior, Mrs. Dawson (Roman Terrace), Mrs. Robson (Denaby), Mrs. Scott, Mrs. Wilson.

The bearers were his particular friends from the New Hope Workingmen's Club, Messrs. J. Searle, Henry Nettleship, Herbert Bratley, and Wm. Bratley.

Wreaths were :-" From his Loving Wife and Children," " Mr. and Mrs. Henry Marrow," " Mrs. Dawson," " Mrs. Marrow and Wilfred." The Rev. I. Middleton officiated.

The coffin was supplied by Mr. J.H. White, and was of parallel pitch pine with brass mounts, inscribed :- John Marrow, Died July 9th 1912, aged 30 years.

James McDonagh
17 Cliff View, Denaby

Funeral – Denaby Cemetery, Saturday.   Priest – Rev. Father Kavanagh

Mourners :- Mrs. McDonagh (widow), Anthony McDonagh (son), Edith and Gertrude McDonagh (daughters), Nora and James McDonagh (son and daughter In-law), Mr. and Mrs. Howley (Goldthorpe) (sister and brother-in-law), Mrs. J. Wagner (sister, Shepherd's Bush, London), Mr. and Mrs. Egan (sister and brother in-law) Bloxwich, Mrs. Durkin and Mrs. Durkin Sen. (Barnsley), Mr. and Mrs. F.K. McDonald (Denaby), Mr. Alf Rudge and Mr. C. Walsh (Denaby), Mr. John Thomas McDonnell (Denaby), Mr. Thos. Housley (Conisbrough) (fellow workmen), Mr. Alf Mills (Bolton on Dearne).
Deceased was borne to the grave by Messrs. John Pigeon, Anthony Pigeon, Wm. Crane, Red Glennon, Edward Collins, Edward Kelley, Martin Carney, and John McHugh.

The coffin was of pitch-pine, inscribed :-" James McDonagh "Died July 10th 1912 aged 49 years. Wreaths :-" From Loving Wife," " Wife and Children," " Edith and Gertrude," " Mrs. F.K. McDonald," " Mrs. Wagner (London)," " Mr. Robson (London.)

Mr. J.H. White, undertaker, carried out the whole arrangements.

The Census in 1911 listed 14 people living at 17 Cliff View:

Person	Relation	Ages	Occupation:	Born
Mcdonagh, James	Head	48	Miner Coal Hewer	Swinsford Co Mayo
Mcdonagh, Kate	Wife (24 Years)	46		Browood Staffs
Mcdonagh, Edith	Daughter	20		Bloxwich Staffs
Mcdonagh, Gertrude	Daughter	18		Bloxwich Staffs
Mcdonagh, Anthoney	Son	16	Miner Pony Driver	Bloxwich Staffs
Mcdonagh, Norah	Daughter	14		Bloxwich Staffs
Mcdonagh, Winifred	Daughter	12	School	Bloxwich Staffs
Mcdonagh, James	Son	7	School	Bloxwich Staffs
Mcdonagh, Agnes	Daughter	4		Denaby Main
Mcdonagh, Kathleen	Daughter	2		Denaby Main
Stephens, Thomas	Boarder	35	Miner Coal Hewer	Kilkearn Galway
Logan, Martin	Boarder	35	Miner Coal Hewer	Kilkearn Galway
Firman, Mark	Boarder	30	Miner Coal Hewer	Creggo Galway
Murry, John	Boarder	36	Miner Coal Hewer	Ballygar Galway

John Mulhearn
22 Adwick Street, Denaby Main

John Mulhearn came from Sheffield and lived with his wife of 6 years, 28 year old Mary Blanche from Huddersfield. They had one child at the 1911 Census, Mary Winifred aged 5.

Martin Mulrooney
Kirby Street, Mexborough.

Martin Mulrooney was a 35 year old Dataller, killed in the first explosion and buried on July 14th. The Rev Kavanagh officiated

Herbert Neal
2 School Terrace, Conisbrough

Funeral – Conisbrough Cemetery, Saturday, 13th July
Minister – Rev. R. Ernest Grieves (Wesleyan).

Mourners :-Mrs. Neal (widow), Mr. W. Neal, Miss V. Neal, Mr. S. and Mr. G. Neal (Louth), Mr. P. Neal, Mr. and Mrs. K. Boldock (Bellean, Lincs), Mr. R. Cook (Tarthwell, Lincs.), Mrs. Marshall (Northcoates), Messrs. Herbert and Harry Brown (nephews), and Ann Neal (niece), Mr. H. Neal (Melbourne, Australia).

Members of the St. John Ambulance Brigade, of which deceased was a member, acted as pall-bearers. The Wesleyan Mission Band was in attendance.
Wreaths from :-" His Wife," " His Father, Brothers and Nephew," " from the Wesleyan Mission Band," and" from Mr. T. Parkes."

At the time of the 1911 Census, Herbert Neal, born in Tathwell, Lincolnshire, was listed as a Fireman and lived with his wife of 13 years Katherine aged 35 who came from Corby in Lincolnshire.

Also living with them was their son, George William, aged 13 and apprentice to a Baker, daughter Violet Annie Neal, aged 7 and brother Frederick Neal aged 27 and employed as a Labourer above ground – all born in Lincolnshire

Herbert Neal's headstone inscription:
The beloved husband of Katherine Neal, of Conisbrough,
who perished in the Cadeby Colliery explosion, July 9th 1912,
aged 33 years
Thy purpose Lord we cannot see
But all is well that's done by Thee
Also of the above named Kathrine Neal
and wife of Fred Neal, his brother,
who died May 5th 1930, aged 54 years

Percy Edgar Nicholson
5 Beech Hill, Conisbrough

The funeral took place on Saturday at the Conisbrough Cemetery, of Percy Edgar Nicholson, who was killed in the recent sad catastrophe at the Cadeby mine. A large number of mourners were present, including :-
Mr. William Nicholson (father), Mrs. Isabella Nicholson (mother), Miss M. Nicholson (sister), Mr. G.W. Nicholson (brother), Miss Minnie Nicholson (niece), Mr. and Mrs. F. Nicholson of Cadeby (uncle and aunt), Mr. T. Nicholson (uncle), Mr. C. Nicholson of Sheffield (uncle), Mr. and Mrs. T. Nicholson of New Cross, Mr. and Mrs. F. Nicholson of Conisbrough (uncle and aunt), Mr. and Miss Walton of Sheffield, Messrs. P. and W. Ackroyd, Mr. and Mrs. Murphin, Mr. and Mrs. Monk, and many others.

The floral tributes included :- A globe from " The Family," A large wreath from " Friends and Neighbours of Beech Hill," and Flowers from " Mrs. Ackroyd of Edlington," and " Mr. H. Appleyard."

The deceased, who was in his 19th year, held the greatest esteem of all his fellow workmen and those with whom he came into daily contact. He had only been back at work a little over a fortnight, since recovering from an attack of typhoid, which occasioned a stay of several weeks at the Conisbrough Isolation Hospital.

We extend our most sincere condolences to the friends and relatives of the deceased.

Jarrett Phillips
12 Wood View, Denaby Main

MINING HEROES' FUNERALS.
On Saturday last the funeral of Mr. Jarratt Phillips, deputy, a hero of the rescue party, took place from his residence, Wood View, Denaby to Conisbrough cemetery.
As the deceased was highly respected by all the workmen who worked under him, they attended in large numbers to show their sympathy, also the officials of No.1 North district, and members of the ambulance class, of which the deceased was a member.

A large number of relatives were present at the funeral Mourners: Mrs. Phillips (widow), Mr. S. Phillips (brother), Mr. P. Winfield, Mr. and Mrs. E. Peters (daughter and son-in-law), Misses Gerty, Laura and Gladys Phillips (daughters), Mr. Leonard Phillips (son), Mrs. Ben Wall (sister), Mr. and Mrs. Meredith (sister and brother-in-law), Mr. and Mrs. B. Whitlam, Mr. Sam Phillips, Miss E. Phillips, Mrs. Nettleton, Mrs. Millwood, Miss Nellie Nettleton, Mr. and Mrs. J. Lunn (Mexborough), Mr. Lewisham, Mr. J. Nettleton, Mr. George Nettleton and Mrs. Nettleton, Mrs. Watson Colton, Mr. D. Smeaton and Miss Annie Smeaton, Mr. and Mrs. A.J. Peters, Mr. F. Willis, Mr. J. Worth, Mr. Wilson, Mr. Mullinew, Mr. J. Wigfield, and Mr. P. Winfield (Denaby).

Bearers – Messrs. A. Sykes, A. Westlake, T. Stones, F. Dows, A. Wilding, W. Hodges, W. Wilkinson and G. Stones.

The coffin was of panelled oak, unpolished with brass fittings, and was borne to the grave by Mr. A. Sykes, Mr. Wilkinson, Mr. W. Hodges, Mr. A. Cusack, Mr. Thomas Stone and Mr. A. Westlake ;members of the ambulance corps.

Some beautiful glass wreaths were sent :-" From his loving Wife and Family," " From his Mother, Sister and Brothers," " From the Officials of No.1 North district Cadeby," A floral wreath was sent from his Brother and Sister, and a harp from his Wife.

The whole of the funeral arrangements were in the hands of J. Millwood, of Mexborough.

William Henry Pickering.
Lawn House, Doncaster

**His Majesty's Chief Inspector Of Mines for Yorkshire and North Midlands
Killed In The 2nd Explosion in Cadeby Main Colliery
July 9th 1912 In His 52nd Year.
He Led The Rescue Party After The 1st Explosion
and By An Act Of Supreme Valour
Crowned a Life Devoted to The Service Of God and
Man by a Heroic Death.**

Why Was It ?
The death of Mr. Pickering was the first to be confirmed, and those who could relapse into anything approaching calmness, on the realisation of the news, did wonder how it was that so gifted a craftsman should have been caught in the toils. Here was lying dead a man of magnificent experience, a man who had run the gauntlet of hundreds of explosions, had forced his way through many hazards, had directed and encouraged and guided in the midst of many perils ; a man who had often risked his life, but never needlessly.

We shall never be given anything like a cogent account of this second explosion. I think, but if there is any reliable narrative to be obtained, we shall want to know whether Mr. Pickering followed his invariable precaution of seeing that the ventilation was kept sound and good, inch by inch, step by step. We cannot suppose that lives were recklessly thrown away on the hands of a seasoned scientist.

A Brilliant Victim.
Mr. Pickering, of whom the Home Secretary, in his telegram of sympathy, spoke in the highest terms, has long been looked upon as one of the leading authorities on coal mining in the whole world. He has, for a considerable number of years occupied the position of Divisional Inspector for Yorkshire and Lincolnshire, with a break of about two years, during which he did similar duty in India, and quite recently won the Edward medal for a signal act of bravery in supporting a doomed miner while he took the sacrament from a priest. One of the painful features of his untimely end is the circumstance that he would have been lunching with the King and Queen at Hickleton Hall at the time he was lying amid the ruins of the second explosion.

Funeral Of Mr. Pickering. Archbishop Officiates
The funeral of Mr. Pickering has been fixed to take place at Doncaster on Saturday afternoon. Canon Sandford (Vicar of Doncaster) and an intimate friend of the deceased gentleman, will officiate. The body of the late Chief Inspector now lies at his residence in Lawn Road, Doncaster. The Edward Medal, he so nobly won, reclines upon his breast.

How The Late Mr. Pickering Won The Edward Medal.
Mr. Pickering, who was the Chief Inspector of Mines for Yorkshire and the North-Midland district, was in his fifty-fourth year. The son of a Wigan gentleman, he was educated at St. Peter's School, York, and after being trained as a mining engineer was placed first in the examination of candidates for inspectorships.

He was appointed assistant inspector in 1866 and spent some years in India as chief inspector of mines. Two years ago he was awarded the Edward Medal of the first class for his bravery in connection with an accident at the Water Haigh Mine, Oulton, near Leeds. Five men were killed, but one, Patrick McCarthy, was pinned by the legs and lingered in agony for several hours.

Mr. Pickering was one of six men who were decorated for endeavouring to save McCarthy. The water rose until it had reached the man's shoulders, and he became delirious, but Mr. Pickering stayed by him at the risk of his own life. Two doctors and a priest were taken down to McCarthy, whose terrible suffering came to an end just as they reached him.

Charles Edward Beswich Prince

The Glen, Mexborough

A Popular Youngster.

One of the most pathetic features of the dreadful aftermath of the week-end, was the recovery from the big fall that followed the second explosion, of the body of Charles Edward Prince, assistant deputy, who lived with his sister Miss E. Prince of The Glen, Harlington Lane, Mexborough, a member of the Mexborough Secondary School staff.

The body was recovered early on Saturday morning, and on Sunday morning it was conveyed to the unfortunate young man's home in Nottinghamshire, in the charge of his sister, and his brother, Walter Prince.

Deceased was a sergeant in the ambulance brigade, and scoutmaster of the Denaby troop of boy scouts. As his coffin was conveyed past Wood View, Denaby Main, a company of nursing women and a squad of ambulance men lined up and respectfully saluted. The coffin was put on the train at Swinton Midland station.

Deceased was formerly associated with the Church Lads Brigade, and was prominent in the Cadeby St. John Ambulance Brigade. District Scoutmaster Mr. G. Donald Gray, of Doncaster, had a most cordial recommendation of Mr. Prince for Scoutmaster's warrant of the 1st Denaby troop from Mr. H.S. Witty. A telegram was sent as follows to the parents of the deceased :- " Deepest sympathy from all Scouts of Doncaster district at death of your heroic son." It is not unlikely that steps will be taken to perpetuate the memory of the deceased in some suitable form.

On Sunday morning, the coffin containing the mortal remains of the deceased was removed from the premises of the Cadeby Main Colliery, where it had been placed for the purpose of identification, to a hearse which was waiting. Upon the coffin were placed exquisite wreaths from his young friends the Scouts, from Mr. and Mrs. Witty, from the Denaby Lawn Tennis Club, from the teachers of Mexborough Secondary School, from the Mexborough Hockey Club, and also from Mrs. Twigg, and other friends. On the coffin lid was also the cap worn by Mr. Prince as Scoutmaster. The procession was headed by members of the Denaby Scout troop, about thirty in number, wearing black scarves or black braid on coat sleeves. The cortege passed through Mexborough about eight o'clock and reached the Swinton Midland station ready for the eight-twenty train.

The members of the Denaby Scout troop stood at 'attention' near the coffin until the train drew up, and, as it was deposited in the special van the 'saluted' remaining very respectfully in that attitude until the train left the station. The early passengers were evidently much impressed by the solemn proceedings. The young scouts kept their excellent control over their feelings until the train passed and then their tears fell unrestrained. Their beloved leader had left them and they fully realised it. It was quite pathetic after they had left the station, to see Patrol-leader Twigg re-form the troop for the return journey. On Sunday afternoon about the time the funeral ceremony was taking place in Nottingham, a memorial service was held in Mexborough Parish

Charles Prince

Church. Scouts were present from Doncaster, Mexborough, Denaby Main, Swinton, Goldthorpe, and Hickleton.

District Scoutmaster Gray of Doncaster was present, and he would have been accompanied by the borough contingent and others from the district, but for a misunderstanding in regard to the train.

There were also present Scoutmasters Spring, Harrison, Gray and Hough, and Assistants Tyas, Woods, Wrigley, Moulton and Stevenson.

The Vicar and Rural Dean, the Rev. W.H.F. Bateman M.A., gave a very good and appropriate address as Chaplain of the Mexborough troop. The rev. gentleman referred to how the deceased promptly attended to the call of duty after the colliery catastrophe, rather than attend a parade at Hickleton Hall. The lessons which he had taught the troop he put into personal practice, and his heroism would long be remembered.

Outside the church Scoutmaster Wild of Goldthorpe, played the 'Last Post.' Scoutmaster Spring very kindly provided tea for all the visiting officers and scouts on the lawn at his residence near the Mexborough National School.

The internment took place at twelve-forty-five in the churchyard of Risley, Nottinghamshire, two miles from 'Sandiacre' the home of the Prince family, and the service was conducted by the Rev. Canon Massey, Vicar of Risley.

The principal mourners included :-Mrs. M. Prince (widow and mother of deceased), Miss E.D. Prince B.A., Miss May Prince, Miss Margaret Prince and Miss Frances Prince (sisters), Mr. James Prince, Mr. Walter Prince, and Master Harold (brothers), Mr. T.W. Ireland M.A. (headmaster Mexborough Secondary School), Miss A.R. Banbury B.A., Mr. and Mrs. A. Huntingdon (Mexborough), and Mr. E. Sutcliffe B.A.

Charles William Phillip Radley

75 Balby Street, Denaby Main

Insurance Company's Generous Action.

Dear Sir

I should like you to report in the columns of your newspaper a generous action on the part of the Prudential Insurance Company. My husband, Charles Radley, who was killed in the Cadeby disaster made a proposal for 2d per week on his life on July 8th and was killed on the 9th. No premium had been paid, and no policy issued, but on the matter being brought before the company by Mr. Townsend of Wath, they generously paid the claim in full. For which I am most thankful.

Yours faithfully

J.M. Radley, 75 Balby Street, Denaby Main.

Frederick Richardson
31 Tickhill Square, Denaby Main.

Funeral – Conisbrough Cemetery, Saturday, 13th July Priest – Rev. W.A. Strawbridge.

Mourners: Mrs. Richardson (widow), Mr. F. Richardson (son), Miss Doris Richardson (daughter), Mr. and Mrs. J. Oates, Mr. H. Richardson (brother), Mrs. E. Hatfield, Mr. James Stead, Mr. F. Brooke, Miss S.A. Brooke, Mr. and Mrs. H. Parker, Mr. and Mrs. Hallas, Mr. and Mrs. Newton, Mr. and Mrs. Brookes, Mrs. Wood, Mrs. Kitson, Mrs. Harwood, Mr. and Mrs. A, Higgins, Mrs. Booth, Mr. G. Booth, Mrs. N.J. Shepherd, Mr. G. Fletcher, Mrs. F. Walker, Mr. T. Maddison, Mr. G. Halmshaw, Mr. T. Slater, and others.

A large number of Conisbrough Druids attended.

Wreaths :- " From Wife and Family," " Mr. and Mrs, Hanley," " Mrs. Bury," " Mrs. Newton," and " Mr. and Mrs. N. Brookes."

Mexborough Times, March 15th, 1913

Children's Claim.

Mary Smith, of 31, Tickhill Street, who had been living with Fred Richardson who was killed, claimed in respect to two children, a son and daughter, now 21 and 11 years.

The applicant said she was a married woman but left her husband Phillip Smith 22 years ago, since when she had been living with the deceased as his wife. He earned 30/- (£1.50) per week. The boy, who was 21, had worked at the pit, but had had to give up owing to ill-health. He was now an insurance agent and earning 13/- (65p) per week Mr. Gichard submitted that there was no total dependency in regard to the son, and with regard to the daughter only partial dependency.

His Honour made the maximum award in respect to the girl, £300, and allowed £5 for current expenses and 12/- (60p) per week. Addressing Mrs. Smith, His Honour said she must give him an undertaking that she would expend the money for the benefit of the child and not for anyone else.

Cyrus Rodgers
48 Ivanhoe Road, Conisbrough

Funeral – Conisbrough Cemetery, Friday, 12th July Priest – Rev. C.P. Mellor.

Mourners :- Mrs. Rogers (widow), Mr. John Rogers (father), Mr. A. Rogers (brother), Mr. W. Robinson, Mr. P. Robinson (brother-in-law), Master Reginald Rogers (son), Mrs. Bennett, Mrs. Warren, Mrs. Sidebottom, Mrs. Ford, Miss Annie Lawrence and Mrs. Lawrence.

Between twenty and thirty of deceased's comrades followed.

Bearers – Messrs. J. Warren, A. Bennett, J. Sidebottom, C. Warren, H. Ford, C. Plum, A. Proctor, and D. Lesley.

Joseph Roodhouse

127 Park Road, Conisbrough

Funeral – Conisbrough Cemetery, Saturday, July 13th   Priest – Rev. W.A. Strawbridge.
Mourners :- Mrs. Roodhouse (widow), Cecil, Mercia, and Horbury, Kathleen and Edgar, Mrs. Roodhouse (mother), Mr. and Mrs. J. Roodhouse, Mr. and Mrs. Lowe, Mr. and Mrs. Clements, Mr. and Mrs. Hill, Mr. and Mrs. Walker, Mr. and Mrs. Roodhouse, and the Misses Roodhouse. Friends from the Socialist Labour Party also attended.
Bearers – Messrs. Longbottom, W. Hague, F. Spencer, Longbottom (2), J. Nuttall.
There was a number of beautiful wreaths.

Joseph Ross

64 Northcliffe, Conisbrough

Amongst the deaths by the explosion was also that of Mr. Ross, of Conisbrough, whose widow is one of the lay preachers on the Primitive Methodist plan, and who is expected to occupy the pulpits at Denaby, Barnburgh and Marr in this quarter. The deceased was a member of the Conisbrough Chapel and was well respected.

Mr. Albert Shakesby, the Evangelist, said that his wife, immediately upon hearing of the explosion, went upstairs to her husband, who had retired to rest, and stated what she had heard, advising him to dress and go to the pit without delay, and see what help he could render. He suggested that his wife might also be of service at the colliery, and she replied, "Yes dear, I will follow on."
He well remembered how willingly the dear woman lent a helping hand to the suffering, and little did she think that her husband had, in the meantime, been carried out of the mine dead. He was sure they all prayed for the Blessing of God upon these and all other mourners.

Joseph lived with his 39 year old wife Sarah Ann and 2 year old daughter Phyliss Ross at the time of the census in 1911

Arthur Edward Rowell

Wadsworth Street, Denaby Main

The remains of Arthur Edward Rowell, one of the victims of the Cadeby explosion, whose body was recovered last Tuesday, were quietly laid to rest at Conisbrough Cemetery yesterday, amidst many manifestations of regret. The service was very impressively conducted by the Rev. S.F. Hawkes .The body was first placed in a shell, and afterwards in a pitch pine coffin with brass mounts, and was carried by Messrs. T. Comer, G. Goulding, J. Norton, T. Hill, F. Crossland, T. Griffiths, J. Armstrong and J. Doran.

The mourners were :-Mrs. Rowell (widow), Florry and Elsie (daughters), Mr. and Mrs. Rowell (father and mother, York), Mr. and Mrs. Kitchen (sister and brother-in-law, York), Mr. and Mrs. Rowell (brother and sister-in-law, York), Mrs. C. Kilner (sister-in-law, York), Mr. and Mrs. Burgoine (Conisbrough), Mr. Kay and Mr. Davis (Denaby).Many beautiful wreaths and flowers were sent by relatives and friends.The funeral arrangements were carried out by Mr. E. Downing of Conisbrough.

Samuel Thomas Sanders
60 Cliff View Road, Denaby Main

Samuel was a 51 year old dataller, who died in the second explosion and was buried at Denaby on July 12th with the Rev Hawke officiating

Headstone:
In loving memory of SAMUEL THOMAS
the beloved husband of CLARA SANDERS
Who gave his life for others in the Cadeby Colliery Disaster,
9th July 1912, aged 51 years
" Greater love hath no Man"
Also of the above named CLARA SANDERS
Who died July 25th 1914 Aged 53 years
"Thy will be done"

Joseph Shuttleworth
5 Cross Street, Conisbrough

Joseph was a 47 year old Corporal who died in the second explosion and was buried at Conisbrough on July 13th, 1912 with the Rev Strawbridge officiating

At the time of the 1911 Census Joseph lived at 17 Ivanhoe Road, with his wife of 7 years, Barbara, aged 35. They had a son Frederick aged 5. All three originated from Donisthorpe, Derby.

John Smith
65 Firbeck Street, Denaby Main

John Smith was a 58 year old collier who died in the first explosion.

James Springthorpe
143 Tickhill Street, Denaby Main

James Springthorpe was a 19 year old Surveyor
In 1911 he lived with his parents, James (aged 43) and Eliza (aged 36). They had been married for 18 years. His father came from Coalville in Leicestershire and his mother from Halifax in Yorkshire. Also in the house was their daughters, Altha (15), Cecelia (11) ands Edna (7), all born in Swinton.
James had another brother, Amos aged 3 who was born in Denaby With them was father in law John Elliott (70) and mother in law Eliza Elliott (64) They also had an adopted son, William Travis Lyons, aged 21 from Barnsley

From The Inquiry
The Coroner announced that James Springthorpe, the deputy of the south district, who had lost a son in the second explosion, and had himself narrowly escaped, was too ill to appear and give evidence, and Mr. Wilson had taken a statement from him.

James Springthorpe (senior)

143 Tickhill Street, Denaby Main

Mexborough Times, March 15th 1913.

THE LAST VICTIM.   Deputy Suddenly Expires.   Effects Of Gas-Poisoning.
The circumstances surrounding the death of James Springthorpe (45), who was found dead in his bed on Tuesday morning, were fully investigated by Mr. Frank Allen (Coroner), in the Institute, Denaby Main, on Wednesday evening.

Died In Bed.
At the outset, the Coroner stated that it appeared that sometime between mid- night on Monday and eight o'clock on Tuesday morning Mr. Springthorpe died in his bed. He went to bed about midnight and slept in an attic, the only other occupant of which was a man named Atkins. When Atkins went to bed deceased was alright, but when he called him about eight o'clock next morning he received no answer. He informed Mrs. Springthorpe, and Dr. McArthur was sent for. The trouble with the deceased had, apparently, been heart disease and asthma. Everybody knew that Springthorpe was in the second explosion which occurred at the Cadeby mine, and it would be necessary for the jury to listen to the evidence and find whether his death was due or in any way attributed to or connected with that explosion.

Memories Of The Explosion.
The first witness called was Mrs. Eliza Springthorpe (widow). Before July 9th last, she said, her husband's health was good. On July 9th, deceased went to work about 4-45 in the morning. He did not then know about the accident, and would not have known about it until he got to the pit. Witness next saw her husband when he was brought home at about 1-30 p.m. in a motor-car. He was then in a very bad state, suffering from internal injuries. Dr, McArthur attended him that evening. Deceased told her that he had been in the explosion at the Cadeby mine.
Since that day her husband had not been well ; he had kept having spasms ever since. . He was able to start work again on the 15th January. He had been afternoon deputy in the South district – the same district as before. He last went to work on Sunday night. His last spasm was on Friday between 2 and 2-30 a.m. On Monday night deceased went to bed about twelve, apparently in his usual health. He slept in an upper room, in which a friend named Joe Atkins, who had come over for the night, occupied a separate bed. On Tuesday morning Atkins came downstairs and told witness her husband was 'funny' and she went upstairs and discovered he was dead. She sent for Dr. McArthur, who arrived between 8 and 8.30.
Mr. H.S. Witty gave evidence to the effect that deceased as deputy, went down with a rescue party between 5 and 6 a.m. He saw him at the top of the pit in a somewhat collapsed condition when he was brought up about twelve noon.

Medical Evidence.
Dr. John McArthur deposed that on July 9th deceased was suffering from burns on his face, arms, body and hips, and had bruises all over his body. He was suffering from shock and gas poisoning. He also complained of a burning sensation in his mouth and throat. Witness attended deceased for the next three months. During the three months he came to the surgery, he complained of shortness of breath and weak action of the heart, known as cardiac asthma. Witness last saw him alive on February 10th. Death was due to heart failure, he could suggest no other cause. The form of poisoning from which deceased was suffering was carbon monoxide.

In his summing up, the Coroner said he had not considered it necessary to enter into the details of the Cadeby mine explosion. What the jury had to consider was the cause of death. After a few minutes deliberation in private the jury returned a unanimous verdict, as follows :-
" Death was due to heart failure, following cardiac asthma, the result of breathing carbon monoxide in the Cadeby Main mine in the explosion of 9th July 1912."

George Steadman, alias Young
86 Blythe Street, Denaby Main,

George Steadman was a 31 year old dataller who died in the first explosion

Mexborough Times, September 28th 1912
On Thursday 21st September remains were identified as those of :- George Steadman alias Young (31), dataller, of 36 Blythe Street, Denaby Main, Considering that the bodies had been entombed in the mine since so far back as July 9th, they were in a remarkably good state of preservation, howbeit the features were more or less unrecognisable.

Mexborough Times, March 15th, 1913
There was another claim in respect to the death of a man named George Young. The applicants were his illegitimate son George Frederick Young aged 12 and the boy's grandfather George Steadman. They live in London.

The deceased man was known at the colliery as George Steadman. Some years ago the deceased miner cohabitated with a girl named Emily Steadman. They were never married, the reason being with the man, said Mr. J. Raley, that he was once in the Army, and left. The girl's reason she would not marry on account of the state of her health. While living together the boy was born. The man for a long time supported both the mother and the boy during the time he was at Denaby. She died two years ago, and the boy was looked after by the woman's father, to whom the deceased often forwarded money.

This man George Steadman, said the deceased had contributed 5s. and 6s. per week to his and the boy's maintenance, but admitted that since January 1912 he had not sent anything. They had to go into the workhouse.

Frederick Stone
39 Warmsworth Street, Denaby Main

Frederick Stone was a 33 year old dataller who came from Liverpool and lived with his wife, 33 year old Hannah from Scunthorpe.

At the time of the Census in 1911 they had 2 daughters Emily aged 1 and Annie aged 2 months.

Frederick died in the second explosion and his body was one of the last to be recovered and was buried on 23rd September – see **William Dove**

Thomas Stribley.
44 Edlington Street, Denaby Main

One of the rescue party who was killed in the Cadeby Pit disaster, July 9th 1912.

Unfortunately, at the time of the explosion we were unable to secure a photograph of Stribley.

We are now pleased to give a reproduction of a photo recently handed to us, in order to give a more permanent record of one who, with others, readily went to the rescue of their unfortunate comrades, and most heroically met their death.

Tom Stribley was a 35 year old dataller who died in the second explosion. He was buried on 12th July at Denaby with the Rev Hawkes officiating

Headstone
The beloved Husband of Annie Stribley
who was accidentally killed
at Cadeby Main Colliery
July 9th 1912
Aged 35 Years
In the midst of life we are in death
He gave his life for others
also Edward the beloved Husband of Sarah Stribley
and father of the bove

Willie Summerscales
25 Tickhill Street, Denaby Main

Willie was a 37 year old deputy killed in the second explosion. His funeral was at Conisbrough Cemetery, Saturday 13th July, Priest Rev. F.S. Hawkes.

Mourners :-Mrs. Summerscales (widow), Rowena, Gwennie, and Phyllis Summerscales (daughters), Mr. and Mrs. Summerscales, Mr. Randolph Summerscales (brother), Councillor and Mrs. W.H. Hurst (Darfield), Mr. and Mrs. Garbutt (brother-in-law and sister), Mrs. Brown (sister), Mr. Ben Fawkes (brother-in-law), Mrs. Atkinson (sister), Sylvester, Gilbert, and Willie Hurst (nephews. Darfield). Bearers – Denaby Druids.

Flowers from widow, Mr. and Mrs. Hurst (Darfield), Mrs. Murray, the officials of the Sheffield Equalised Independent Druids, Mrs. Fawkes, Mrs. Atkin, Mr. W.H. Gibbs, and Mr. Brough.

Timothy Smith Talbot
125 Tickhill Street, Denaby Main

The funeral of the late Mr. Timothy Smith, of Ashby-de-la-Zouch, Leicester, took place on July 12th, 1912

The deceased was well-known in Leicestershire musical circles, having attained some prominence in that county as a teacher of music. He was an expert organist, having been, we believe, a pupil of the celebrated Dr. Plant of Burton.

He came to work at the Cadeby mine some four weeks ago, and was a victim of the unfortunate disaster.

There were a large number of family mourners, and a large concourse of sympathisers assembled.

Timothy was a 28 year old filler, killed in the second explosion

John William Tarbrook

30 Firbeck Street, Denaby Main

John William Tarbrook lived with Annie Rodgers aged 28, under the name of Ms Tarbrook John William came from Stannington and Annie from Bradley in Derbyshire. John's age at the 1911 Census is shown as 25.

Mexborough Times, March 15th, 1913
His Honour Judge Allen, on Monday, at a special sitting at the Doncaster County Court, was asked to arbitrate on two very interesting cases arising out of the Cadeby disaster. The applicants in the first case were two infants, John Frederick Tarbrook, and Irene Tarbrook, and the respondents were the Denaby and Cadeby Collieries Ltd. and William and Mary Tarbrook, of 216 Malin Bridge Road, Sheffield, who claimed partial dependency.

Mr. T.E. Ellison, instructed by Mr. J. Raley, explained that the two infants were two years and three months old respectively, and were the illegitimate children of a man named John Wm. Tarbrook, now deceased, who was a miner, earning an average wage of 28s per week, and was twenty three years of age. On the 9th of July last, when there was a disastrous explosion at the Cadeby Colliery, he volunteered for rescue work, and he lost his life being suffocated and burnt. The facts relating to the children were that in 1910 the deceased man became acquainted with a married woman, named Annie Rodgers, who had left her husband because of his ill-treatment. She went to live with the deceased, and in September 1910 they went to live at Denaby. According to the evidence from that time until his death they lived happily together under the name of Mr. and Mrs. Tarbrook, and were reputed to be man and wife. On the 11th March 1911, the eldest child John Frederick was born and was registered by the deceased woman. The other child was born three months after her father's death.

Henry Thompson

2 Sprotborough Street, Denaby Main

The funeral took place at Mexborough Cemetery on Friday, 12th July. Deceased was very well-known in the district, and leaves a widow and one child to mourn his loss. The Rev. W.H.F. Bateman officiated. The chief mourners were :- Mrs. Hy. Thompson (widow), Emily, Mr. and Mrs. Thomas Thompson (father and mother), Mr. William Thompson, Mr. and Mrs. Pope, Mr. Wilfred Thompson, Mr. and Mrs. Thomas Bovell, Mr. S. and J. Bovell, Mr. and Mrs. R. Schofield, Mr. and Mrs. Bodkin, Mr. and Mrs. J. Burns, Mr. Fred Crowson.

Henry Thompson was a 21 year old Filler, killed in the first explosion

James Thompson
6 Adams Yard, Mexborough.

The funeral took place on Friday at the Mexborough Cemetery, the Rev. W. H.F. Bateman officiating.
The mourners were :- Mrs. Thompson (widow), Mrs. Nettleship (daughter), Miss Elsie Thompson and Miss Ethel Thompson (daughters), Mr. and Mrs. Metcalf (Middletown), Mr. and Mrs. Lomas (Wombwell), Mr. and Mrs. Wallwork from (Manchester),Mr. and Mrs. Thompson (Wombwell), Mrs. J. Fairhurst (Wombwell), Mr. S. Fairhurst (Worsborough Dale), Miss Annie Lomas and Miss J. Richardson (Wombwell), Mrs. E. Brown, Miss T. Ellis (Mexborough).
The bearers were – Messrs. C. Wotton, J. Chadbourne, J. Reynolds, H. Platts, J. Landale, and W. Crowther.
Wreaths from :-" Wife ", " Mrs. Nettleship," " Elsie and Ethel Thompson," " Miss Kate Ellis," " Mr. and Mrs. J. Thompson," " Mrs. Brown," and other friends.
Mr. J.H. White, undertaker, carried out the whole funeral arrangements.

James Thompson was a 54 year old dataller also killled in the first explosion.

Gilbert Young Tickle
548 Ecclesall Road, Sheffield

The late Mr. G.Y. Tickle
H.M. Junior Inspector of Mines
Few incidents connected with the Cadeby disaster present a more tragic aspect than the heroic and untimely end of Mr. G.Y. Tickle. He was 34 years of age and was appointed Inspector in August 1909, being first stationed in Sheffield, then in Leeds, and for the past 12 months in Doncaster as Mr.Pickering's personal assistant. During his stay in Yorkshire he has gained the very highest esteem of all with whom he came into contact, both on account of his personal characteristic and professional ability. He was one of the honorary secretaries of the Doncaster Engineering Society, and his efforts i will be greatly missed.

He was born in Liverpool in 1877 and was educated at the Merchant Taylors School and at George Watson College, Edinburgh. He was articled to Messrs. J. and G.H.Geddes, Mining Engineers, of the latter city, and received his practical training at the colleries belonging to his grandfather's firm, Messrs Nimmo and Son Limited of Glasgow. Prior to his appointment as Inspector he spent several years in the Lancashire Coalfield.

In temperament Mr.Tickle was deliberate and undemonstrative; but all who knew him testify with enthusiasm to his generosity of heart and mind. He was conspicuously devoted to the duties of his profession, the exacting demands iof which prevented his participating freely in the social life of the town.

On the morning of the disaster he was on his way to Barnsley Main Colliery to investigate the cause of an accident, but hearing of the explosion at Cadeby he went straght to the spot and nobly sacrificed his life in the hope of saving his fellows.

The interment took place at Eastwood Cemetery, Glasgow on Friday.

Home Secretary's Message.

From the Secretary of State, (addressed to Mr. Redmayne, Chief Inspector of Mines at Cadeby)

The Home Secretary is greatly shocked at the death of the three inspectors, Pickering, Hewitt and Tickle, and the others in the disaster at Cadeby Main. Will you make known to the relatives and at the mine, his deep sympathy and concern in this great sorrow, and his admiration for the heroism of the men who hazarded their lives to work in the rescue.

The Home Secretary feels it impossible to measure the extent of the loss that his department has suffered by the death of one of the ablest and most experienced inspectors and his two devoted colleagues.

Charles Edgar Tuffrey   Edmund Jesse Tuffrey

30 Northcliffe Road, Conisbrough

Funeral at Conisbrough Cemetery, Saturday 13th July. Minister – Rev. T. Mallard.

Mourners:- Mr. G. Tuffrey, Messrs. C. and A. Tuffrey, Elsie and Phyllis, Mr. and Mrs. E. Tuffrey, Miss P. Barker, Miss M. Monks, Mr. and Mrs. Green (Barnsley), Mr. Allen, Mr. Lovell (Donisthorpe), Mr. Joseph Scott

Members of the St. John Ambulance Brigade also followed.
Friends of the deceased acted as bearers.
Wreaths from:- " Father, Brothers and Sisters.,", " Mr. and Mrs. A. Goacher (Donisthorpe)," " Mrs. E. Lovell (Enderley)," " Miss P. Barker," " Miss May Monks," " Mr. G. Broughton," " Mr. J. Spratt," " Mr. and Mrs. Tuffrey."

Detail from the 1911 Census when the family lived at 61 Gardens Lane, Conisbrough:

Name:	Relationship	Age	Occupation:	Birth Place
Tuffrey, George C.	Head	44	Coal Miner	Oxon, Thrupp
Tuffrey, Mary A.	Married 22 Yrs	45		Oxon, Islip
Tuffrey, Edmund J.	Son	20	**Coal Miner**	**Oxon, Weston On The Green**
Tuffrey, Charles E.	Son	19	**Coal Miner**	**Oxon, Weston On The Green**
Tuffrey, Elsie B.	Daughter	17		Oxon, Weston On The Green
Tuffrey, Cyril H.	Son	11	School	Leics, Moira
Tuffrey, Phyllis M.	Daughter	7	School	Leics, Moira
Tuffrey, Albbert O.	Son	3		Leics, Donisthorpe
Scott, Joseph H.	Boarder	19	Coal Miner	Leics, Donisthorpe

Joseph Turner
66 Warmsworth Street, Denaby Main

Joseph Turner was a 26 year old Dataller. He was buried on 13th July, 1912 with Rev Smith officiating

William Henry Wallace
14 Barmborough Street, Denaby Main

Funeral – Denaby Cemetery, Saturday, 14th July Priest – Rev. S.F. Hawkes.

Mourners :- Mrs. Wallace (widow), Mr. and Mrs. W. Wallace, Mr. and Mrs. Fisher (Bolton), Mr. and Mrs. Griffin (Bolton), Mr. and Mrs. Knock, Mr. and Mrs. J. Alderman Crokworth, Miss C. Wallace, Mr. and Mrs. Wallace (Fitzwilliam Village), Misses Bagshaw and Fisher, and J. Wallace.

The coffin was borne to the grave by members of the Salvation Army.
There were a number of beautiful floral tributes

William Wallace was born in Leicestershire 1856, he was the eldest son of Irish immigrants Patrick Wallace and Margaret (Fitzsimons) Wallace. His wife Elizabeth (nee Lowe) was born in Nottinghamshire 1855.

Elizabeth never remarried and survived her husband by twenty three years before her death in 1934, she was seventy nine years old.

(from Sue Hodgson grandaughter of Mr & Mrs Griffin)

William Wallace was a 56 year old Dataller who died in the second explosion. In the 1911 Census and at the time of his death William was living at 14 Barmbrough Street, also living there at the time was was his wife Elizabeth, their son Walter Wallace aged 16 years, and their granddaughter Lydia Wallace aged 5 years.

Thomas Walsh
7 Wood View, Denaby Main

Funerals Of Cadeby Victims.
The funeral of the late Thomas Walsh took place at the Catholic Church on the 13th July 1912

The chief mourners were :- M. Walsh (brother), W. McIntyre (nephew), Mr. and Mrs. Davis, Mr. S. Davis, Miss E. Davis, Misses Gertie, Lily and Minnie Davis, Mr. and Mrs. Malloy, Mr. and Mrs. Riley, Mr. and Mrs. Crump, Mr. and Mrs. Hall, and other friends.

The Rev. Father Kavanagh officiated.

Thomas Walsh was a 41 year old Dataller who died in the first explosion

Frank Walton
10 Strafforth Terrace, Denaby Main

Frank Walton, a 39 year old deputy, who went down with the rescue party and lost his life, was buried by the side of his father on Saturday in Dodworth Churchyard.

The coffin was carried from his residence in Denaby Main to Conisbrough Station by his fellow workmen, who accompanied the remains to Dodworth, and bore them to the grave.

There was a large and sympathetic crowd at Dodworth, people lining the whole distance to the churchyard, where the coffin was met by the Vicar, the Rev. W. S. Barker M.A.

There was a large number of wreaths from, Denaby, Cadeby, and Dodworth.

Benjamin Ward

1 Tickhill Street, Denaby Main

Benjamin Ward was a 30 year old Collier who died in the second explosion.

William David Waters

28 Firbeck Street, Denaby Main

On Sunday, 14th July at Denaby Cemetery, Rev. S.F. Hawkes officiating, the burial of William David Waters took place.
Mourners :-Mrs. Waters (widow), Mr. W. Waters (father), Elizabeth and Anne Waters (children), Ammio Dennis (step-sister), Mrs. Dennis (mother-in-law), Harry Rose, Mrs. Haskey, Mr. and Mrs. Carr.
Wreaths from :- " Widow and Children," " Father, Mother-in-Law," " Mrs. Preston (step-sister)," " Mr. and Mrs. Hollingsworth."
Bearers – Messrs. J. Ellison, T. Smith, R. Mallett, F. Holdsworth, H. Wood, and Jim Holt.

William was a 31 year old Driver who died in the second explosion.

Samuel Webster

19 Ivanhoe Road, Conisbrough

Amongst those killed by the colliery explosion was 41 year old Samuel Webster, a deputy who expired in the seond explosion. He was a member of the Primitive Methodist Chapel, and was a lay preacher in the Mexborough Circuit. He was planned to preach on the 28th inst. at Conisbrough and at Mexborough Chapel next September. He was highly respected and much sympathy is felt for his widow and family.

The internment took place on Friday at Rotherham, and the circuit was represented by Bro. J. Smith, of Mexborough (who rendered good ambulance work at the colliery), Bro. H. Florence and Bro. H. Murphy (of Goldthorpe), three lay preachers.

The service was conducted by the Rev. H. Oliver, superintendent of the circuit, who spoke appropriately in regard to the excellent character of the deceased, and his good work as a member and official of that denomination.

George Whitton

24 Maltby Street, Denaby Main

Funeral Of A Cadeby Victim.   The Late Mr. G. Whitton.
The funeral of one of the victims of the Cadeby disaster took place at Denaby on Friday 12th July, the Rev. S.F. Hawkes officiated. The deceased was George Whitton a 32 year old Deputy and a popular figure in Denaby, being a member of the Ambulance Brigade, and also a member of the Ambulance Band for over six years. There was a large attendance of mourners including :-
Mrs. G. Whitton (widow), Elsie, Elizabeth, John, George, Irinie, and Austin Whitton (children), Mr. and Mrs. Sewell (father and mother-in-law), Mr. and Mrs. Sewell, Mrs. Cutts (Rotherham), Mr. and Mrs. Vickers, Mr. and Mrs. Flinders, Mr. and Mrs. Sewell, Mr. and Mrs. Maurice (Maltby), Harry Maurice, Harry and Elizabeth Maurice (Mexborough), Mr. and Mrs. Holmes (Denaby), Mr. and Mrs. S. Panton, Mr. and Mrs. Jeffcote (Denaby), Mrs. Smalley, Mrs. Liversedge, Mrs. Mullins & Mrs. Stead (Mexborough), Mrs. Clarke (Melton), Mr. Bramham,

Mr. T. Bunting, Mr. H. Bunting, Mr. W. Bunting (Mexborough), Mr. and Mrs. Pearson (West Melton), and a large number of other friends and relatives.

The Denaby Ambulance Band attended, and played the 'Dead March', and 'The Last Call'. The Ambulance Brigade also attended in full.

A large number of wreaths were received, including the following : Wife and Family, Mother and Father, Sisters, Mr. Maurice (Maltby), Mr. Barrington Seed (Doncaster), Mrs. Hurst (Doncaster).

Flowers from neighbours and friends.

Mr. Whitton and family desire to thank all friends and relatives for the many messages of sympathy in their sad bereavement, and also to thank the nursing staff at the hospital.

Thomas Samuel Williams
55 Maltby Street, Denaby Main

Thomas Samuel Williams was a 36 year old deputy and widower living with his sons, Samuel Johnson (12) and Harold William (10) and daughters, Evelyn Beatrice (9) and Anne Elizabeth (6). His sons and Evelyn were born in East Dean, Gloucester and Anne Elizabeth was born in Hereford. To add to the tragedy Thomas had 2 more children as a letter to the Trustees revealed:

Church of England,
Homes for Waifs & Strays, Kennington Road, London

24th July 1912
Dear Sir,
I do not like to trouble you, but I feel it is only right I should acquaint you of the fact, in case you have not already been informed, that the late Mr. Thomas Samuel Williams, who I understand was one of the victims in the recent mine disaster at Cadeby, had two little daughters under this Society's care. The girls are Vera & Rhona; their ages are five and four years respectively; and at the present moment are inmates of our St.Agnes' Home, Mirfield, Yorks.
I should perhaps add that during the man's lifetime he contributed towards the support of the children to the extent of 3/6 (17 1/2p) per week for each child, and as, of course, this amount will be no longer forthcoming, it has occurred to me that possibly your Company may be able to see its way to allocate a certain proportion of the Compensation money, which I presume the relatives of the deceased man are entitled to, to the Society for the support of the two girls referred to. Perhaps therefore, you will kindly let me hear from you on this matter, at your early convenience.
I hope you will not think that this application is too premature as naturally the Society feels it must obtain the assistance, which the little ones can justly claim on the death of their father, in view of the fact that we are now faced with the responsibility of maintaining the two children until they become self-supporting, and also having regard to the many calls on our some-what limited resources.
Awaiting your reply, Believe me,
Yours faithfully E de M Rudolph

Richard Wimpenny

16 Tickhill Square, Denaby Main

Funeral – Conisbrough Cemetery, Saturday 12th July. Minister – Mr. E.W. Oaten (Spiritualist).

Mourners :- Mrs. Wimpenny (widow), Mrs. Wimpenny (mother), Mr. and Mrs. E. Wimpenny, Mr. and Mrs. H. Rogers (daughter and son-in-law), Master Lodge Rogers, Master Richard Rogers (grandchildren), Mr. Wimpenny, Mrs. Speight, Mr. and Mrs. H. Wimpenny, Mr. G. Wimpenny, Mr. and Mrs. T.H. Mills, Mr. and Mrs. S. Senior, Mr. Lodge, Mrs. Hall, Mrs. Denton, Mrs. Jones, Mr. and Mrs. G. Appleby (Sheffield), Mr. W. Appleby, Mr. H. Mills, Mr. Ben Mills, Miss Alice Mills, Mr. and Mrs. A. Wheeliker.

A large number of workmen and Spiritualist friends followed, also the Conisbrough Working-men's Co-operative Society Committee. Deceased was also associated with the Fullerton Hospital. He was most highly respected in the district. The bearers were deceased's fellow workmen.

Wreaths from :- " Family, Brothers and Sister," " Mrs. Hall," "Mr. and Mrs. Lodge," " Mr. and Mrs. A. Webster," " Mr. and Mrs. Denton," " Committee and Members of the Conisbrough Co-operative Society," " Denaby Main officials and workmen," " Mexborough Spiritualist Society," " Mrs. Bury (Red House),"

Richared Wimpenny was a 56 year old deputy who expired in the second explosion

Frank Wood

Braithwell Street, Denaby Main

Frank Wood of Braithwell Street, Denaby Main committed suicide by drowning himself in the River Don on the Saturday following the disaster. His widow gave evidence that her husband had no trouble before the colliery explosion in which he had lost a brother in law.

On Wednesday he had worked down the pit on the task of stretchering out the bodies. On returning home he had said to his wife that the sight was horrible.'I shall never forget it; if I live to be a hundred; I shall never go down the pit again'

He never slept in his bed again.'He would just come home, take a cup of tea and say; I will look sharp down to our Mary's to comfort his widowed sister'.

Thomas Wraithmell

17 Tickhill Square, Denaby Main

Thomas Wraithmell was a 53 year old Onsetter who died in the second explosion and was buried on 13th July 1912.

At the 1911 Census, Thomas Wraithmell was living with his wife of 26 years, Rachel aged 51. Their family consisted of son Cyril (19), a clipper in the Coal Mine and a daughter Dora aged 23. Also in the house was his brothers wife Martha Ann (55) and grand daughter Ethel Wraithmell aged 4 months. Finally 2 boarders, Dennis Summerscales (49) and Marlborough Lunn (28) lived with them

Poems and Songs about the Disaster

This song was released by the Leeds Mercury for the fund for the relief of the widows, orphans and dependants of the victims of the Cadeby Coliery disaster

HEROES OF THE PIT

There are songs about our Soldiers,
the men who guard our land,
There are songs about our Navy,
a gallant hearty band,
But what about our miners
Those heroes down be-low,
Who yield to none in valour,
those men who make no show.

For its down among the coal
that you'll find the purest gold,
Great Britain's best we call them,
those miners strong and bold,
Heroes of the pit are they.
Yes, heroes true and brave,
Aye! heroes ever ready
A comrades life to save.

CHORUS

When the Davy lamp burns blue,
They are dauntless brave and true,
You'll hear their steady tramp
Through the deadly after damp
For they've gone to seek a mate,
Tho its death may be their fate,
Yes its heroes that they are
With their shovel, pick and bar

And when we are safe on land,
They're at work that noble band,
To rescue one from death,
They will fight with baited breath,
There's no quitting of their post
If there is one poor soul still lost
They are heroes every one,
Though they've neither sword nor gun

Rest after Toil

Lines composed by Mr.E.H. Smith, the Blind Evangelist and Founder of the open Air Rescue Mission, Sheffield, out of respect for the poor Cadeby miners

It was down Cadeby mine,
poor men were toiling there
they knew not their danger and death was so near
they left homes and loved ones,
their bread for to gain
and hoping that morn they would see them again

It was early next morning, sad news filled the air
Poor wives and the children in grief and despair
they rushed to that pit yard, their sorrow was great
Amidst bitter tears for their loved ones they wait

Through that sad explosion the men lose their lives
The breadwinner lost leaving children and wives
to fight through the world with great sorrow and pain
May God grant these loved ones
will meet once again

Brave hearts to the rescue soon volunteered to go
without hesitation they went down below
amidst smoke and dust they sought for those lost
they struggled so bravely, their lives it has cost

Then, doctors and nurses they soon hurried there
Amidst dead and wounded their sorrows did share
they lay those poor men in the pay office near
the crowd was so great and shed many a tear

Our dear sovereign the King and the Queen
soon were there
and shared in their sorrows with many a tear
the crowd tried to cheer them as they went past
but the gloom was so heavy
through that great mass

Nearer my God to thee, nearer to thee
let our King and Queen still be nearer to thee
in all the miners be nearer my God to thee
nearer my God to thee, draw us near to thee

Chorus

Brave miners beware, dear miners prepare
you know there are dangers
while toiling down there

Conisbrough's Royal Visit
8th of July, 1912

King George V and Queen Mary came to
Conisbrough.
They called at the castle near the river Don.
Just across the water stood Cadeby Main Colliery,
Their visit was a happy one.

Singing, dancing and laughing.
Good-natured crowds were in jubilation
To have a visit from the King and Queen,
The monarchs of our nation.

The King admired a good deal of what he saw
As he walked around the top of the castle keep
From the town, industry, wood and farmland,
To the cattle and the grazing sheep.

Our monarch descended the castle
He walked over the lawn to the marquee.
It is here he rejoined his lovely Queen Mary
Together with their guests they enjoyed tea.

Many miners, their wives and children
Came out to welcome the royals that day.
The merriment would continue,
Until the royals went on their way.

This happy Monday now over.
The King and Queen had raised a smile.
Some went back to their work at the Colliery.
Some miners stayed out of work for a while.

As time moves on into tomorrow,
Who is to know what tomorrow may bring.
Till then it's good night and God bless to everyone
God save the Queen and King.

Cadeby Main Colliery Disaster
9th of July, 1912

It was the early hours of the morning
As the Dearne Valley lay calm and still,
When a terrible explosion rocked Cadeby Main
Colliery.
The alarm was raised and the pit's siren let out a
shrill.

37 miners worked the colliery's south district
to keep their families clothed and fed.
35 miners paid their terrible price for coal,
now 35 miners were dead.

The rescue teams came quickly,
But little were they to know,
Some hours later that morning –
A crowning blast would follow.

The second explosion engulfed the rescuers
A roof fall and gas killed 53 more.
If it were not for the Conisbrough royal visit.
The death toll could easily have doubled that
score.

King George V and Queen Mary came to the
Cadeby Main Colliery,
Where 88 miners had died.
There were estimated 80,000 mourners
Even our dear Queen Mary cried.

Three more men it is said died later
The final death toll rose to 91.
We shall never forget any miner killed by tragedy,
As we pray for them all everyone.

R.I.P

Poems by Stephen C. Pratt former Miner at Cadeby Main and member of Memorial Committee

In loving memory of the miners and rescuers who lost their lives in the terrible explosion

In health and strength they left their home,
not thinking death so near:
It please the Lord to bid them come
And in his sight appear

Death to them short warning gave
Therefore be careful how you live
Prepare in time, make no delay,
For who made know their dying day.

In prime of life they were cut down,
no longer could they stay;
because it was the Saviour's will,
To call them hence away.

They have gone – a grave has received them
Twas Jesus who called them away;
they have gone to the Lord who redeemed them
from night to the splendour of day

Anon 1912

Memorial Most Worthy

The tolerance of love holds sway over tragedy passing
Still strong in hearts, since its dawn came unpaged
Its memory unending, ten decades now amassing
When the anger of mining thundered and raged

Merciless with intent its fiery temper ignited
No mortal or other could withstand its will
To road stall and gate advanced cruelly uninvited
And black dust laid its shroud in the silence of still

In terrible seconds mining dangers ran amok
The cold finger of tragedy revealed the sad cost
Amid twisted steel, timber, choking dust and rock
The terror of the aftermath gave count to the lost

Alarm heralded the brave, human moles of dedication
The courage of rescuers in haste took the task
To the black depths of hell, with no hesitation
They sought living or perished, what more could one ask

In that muted calm, further disaster hung pending
Then in terrible rage ignited its murderous intent
The gallantry of rescuers lay perished and ending
Their duty bound bravery now fruitless and spent

Yet mines hold no mercy, no sympathy or shame
To invasion of need their dangers hold fast
Now twice the head count in that dark domain
Eighty eight lost souls that count was cast

A cataract of tears over spilled an ocean of despair
The sorrow of the fatalities spoke the guilt of rages
Kin witnessed their ascent in safe hands of care
Such sorrowful scenes would find history pages

Disaster manifests itself in life's resting place
As tear stained masses complete a human epitaph
Heart felt prayers were etched on each and every face
Surely the lost were treading God's heavenly path

Brotherhood's strong bond, shall ne'er decay of neglect
For fallen brothers its need was truly thus born
This day in prayer we will voice heart felt respect
May God's infinite light greet this memorial dawn

We shall not tire to the count of the years
The lost souls must know our measure of sorrow
And if heaven be kind they will witness our tears
Not just for this day but for every tomorrow

Benny Wilkinson

Cadeby Main Colliery Memorial Group

The Cadeby Main Colliery Memorial Group was formed in March 2011.

Aim of Group
The aim of the Group is to provide a permanent memorial to all the men and boys who perished in the Cadeby Main Disaster on July 9th 1912

The Memorial will be the Centrepiece of the Denaby Cemetery and will be inaugurated at the Dedication and Remembrance Day to be held on **July 8th 2012.**

Meetings
Meetings normally take place on the Third Tuesday of each month at the Denaby and Cadeby Miners Welfare Club, Tickhill Square, Denaby Main

Contacts:
Chairman : Jeff Lovell 01709 865522
Secretary : Jim Beachill 07886 718719

Activities
The Group are activly involved in raising money for the Memorial. They have arranged Concerts, Collections and are selling Badges and Calendars as well as this book for this purpose.

The Activities, Meeting Minutes and Progress towards their goal can be seen on the Conisbrough & Denaby Main Local History Web Site:

https://sites.google.com/site/conisbroughlocalhistory/home

John Gwatkin and Jeff Lovell at the Thornycroft Gala